THE LONDON ENGLISH LITERATURE SERIES

General Editor: A. V. C. SCHMIDT M.A.

MEASURE FOR MEASURE

WILLIAM SHAKESPEARE

MEASURE
FOR MEASURE

Edited by
J. G. SAUNDERS B.A. B.LITT.

UNIVERSITY OF LONDON PRESS LTD

ISBN 0 340 11840 7

First published in this edition 1971

Introduction, Commentary, and Notes
University of London Press Ltd
St Paul's House, Warwick Lane, London EC4P 4AH

Printed and bound in Great Britain by
Richard Clay (The Chaucer Press), Ltd, Bungay, Suffolk

CONTENTS

INTRODUCTION

ACCORDING to an entry in the Revels Accounts, a play 'Caled Mesur for Mesur' by 'Shaxberd' was presented at court on 26 December 1604. It is generally accepted that this was the first performance of *Measure for Measure* and that it was written by Shakespeare shortly after King James I's accession to the English throne in 1603.

Although *Measure for Measure* is often classified as a 'problem play' critics have differed considerably in their attempts to define what it is about the play which is problematical. It used to be thought that the 'problem' was Shakespeare's, and that with the other 'problem plays' (*Hamlet, Troilus and Cressida* and *All's Well that Ends Well*) *Measure for Measure* was written during a period in which Shakespeare was disillusioned with life and obsessed by the ugliness of sex. This biographical theory is now generally discredited. More recently these plays have been termed 'problem plays' only because they raise serious moral problems against realistic settings. However, some critics consider that *Measure for Measure* presents an additional problem in that it is artistically flawed. The introduction which follows is divided into two sections. The first section examines Shakespeare's treatment of the 'problems' which sex, authority and death impose on human conduct. The second section deals with the artistic 'problem' and attempts to interpret the play in the light of our knowledge of Elizabethan theatrical conventions. (The term 'Elizabethan' is used throughout this introduction to cover both the reign of Queen Elizabeth and the first years of the reign of King James I.)

I

The World of Romantic Comedy

In his better known 'romantic' comedies Shakespeare had created artificial worlds in which his audience could enjoy a momentary escape from life in an ever-expanding London beset by plague, poverty, overcrowding and unemployment. The enchanting worlds of plays like *A Midsummer Night's Dream, As You Like It* and *Twelfth Night* result from Shakespeare's delicate blending of language, character and setting. *A Midsummer Night's Dream* is set in part in a fairy-haunted wood near an Athens ruled over by a mythological Duke, Theseus; *As You Like It* in a pastoral Forest of Arden which becomes the idyllic backdrop to the romantic entanglements of shepherds and shepherd-esses; and *Twelfth Night* in Illyria, an imaginary country ruled over by a love-sick Duke.

The World of Measure for Measure

In striking contrast to the exquisite artificiality in these earlier plays, the world of *Measure for Measure* is created with an uncompromising realism. Nominally the setting is Vienna, but it is a Vienna which contemporary audiences would have found very like their own London (see *Commentary* 8, 9 and 17). In this city strict laws controlling individual freedom have long been disregarded with the result that liberty has given way to licence. Shortly before he abandons his disguise in the final scene, the Duke tells the assembled inhabitants:

> My business in this state
> Made me a looker-on here in Vienna,
> Where I have seen corruption boil and bubble
> Till it o'er-run the stew.

The corruption has been general, but Shakespeare represents it by concentrating on one particular aspect: sex. 'Stew' meant 'brothel' as well as 'cauldron', and a number of scenes are devoted to an elderly bawd, Mistress Overdone, her pimp, Pompey, and their clients, Lucio, Froth and the two Gentlemen. Pompey and Mistress Overdone live at the heart of the corruption in Vienna. They 'buy and sell men and women like beasts' and have to be restrained from doing so. For, to the Elizabethans, sexual licence meant infection. This fact is repeatedly emphasized in the second scene of the play, the scene in which the sexual disorder in Vienna is most vividly realized. 'I have purchased as many diseases under her roof as come to——' Lucio announces to his companions when Mistress Overdone first enters.

He and his friends joke about their sexual freedom but they dwell continually on venereal disease and its concomitants, bone-ache, baldness and sciatica, and this gives their wit a certain hollowness. Lucio's humour is more than simple comic relief: we are constantly reminded of the sordidness of the setting which is integral to the serious issues raised in the play.

THE PROBLEM OF SEXUAL MORALITY

In different ways, Claudio, Isabella and Angelo are all, like Lucio, products of their environment, and the sexual licence in Vienna has shaped both their lives and their philosophies. When Angelo, on having the Duke's authority delegated to him, revives a long-neglected law enabling him to condemn Claudio to death for fornication, these characters are made to confront each other and themselves in a succession of scenes presented with a degree of realism and psychological insight unparalleled in any of Shakespeare's comedies and rivalling in intensity the most passionate moments in his great tragedies.

Claudio

Although it is Claudio who is condemned to death for fornication, he has been least affected by the moral climate of Vienna. At first his offence seems to be symptomatic of the generally 'permissive' attitude to sex: he is a friend of Lucio and an acquaintance of Mistress Overdone. However, we find that his sleeping with Julietta was not what Lucio would call 'a game of tick-tack', a casual sexual act committed merely to gratify his lust. The couple had been secretly engaged but were delaying their marriage in the hope that by gaining the consent of Julietta's relatives before marrying they would obtain a dowry. Both Claudio and Julietta are deeply penitent and consider that their lack of self-control was sinful. In fact, considering the venial nature of his sin, Claudio's remorse may seem to be excessive if we ignore a psychological truth: that the intensity of guilt is often as much related to the severity of censure and punishment as to the gravity of the offence which occasioned it. In succumbing to desire Claudio has unwittingly brought about not only imprisonment and imminent death for himself, but also public shame for the girl he loves and a complete separation from her and the child. Moreover, an environment like Vienna produces extreme reactions, and when Lucio asks him what has led to his imprisonment, his answer contains an image which expresses both his self-disgust and his disgust with human nature in general. He tells Lucio:

> Our natures do pursue,
> Like rats that ravin down their proper bane,
> A thirsty evil; and when we drink, we die.

Rats were carriers of plague. To destroy them they were fed ratsbane, a powder which induced an uncontrollable thirst but which solidified inside them when they drank water. Shakespeare uses this fact to draw a powerful analogy between the thirst of the rat and the human sexual drive. (The same idea is the basis of one of his most passionate sonnets, 'The expense of spirit in a waste of shame'.) For Claudio the anticipation of sexual pleasure had been sweet, but its gratification has led to his death sentence. However, in speaking of 'our natures' he speaks not only for himself and Lucio but for all mankind. In the words of the Provost: 'All sects, all ages smack of this vice'. And to the Elizabethans, although the driving force of lust was a 'bane' to mankind, it was his 'proper' bane, one from which he could not escape.

For the Elizabethans accepted the medieval notion that Man was suspended in the great chain of God's creation between Angel and Beast, and that he comprised elements of both. The intellectual, immortal part of him, his soul, was angelic; his sensual, mortal body, bestial. Claudio's rat image fittingly indicates his reluctant acceptance of the animality inherent in him.

Angelo

Angelo, as his name implies, seems to have no bestial part to his nature, and in Vienna he is therefore regarded as the epitome of virtue. When the Duke asks Escalus if he considers Angelo worthy to rule in his place, Escalus replies:

> If any in Vienna be of worth

> To undergo such ample grace and honour,
> It is Lord Angelo.

and the Duke himself seems to approve of his behaviour, telling him:

> There is a kind of character in thy life
> That to th'observer doth thy history
> Fully unfold.

However, before giving him his commission, the Duke tells Angelo that true virtue is an active quality derived from Heaven, and he implies that Angelo has been wasting his virtue on himself, in an almost narcissistic way.

To some observers the 'character' in Angelo's life is austere beyond saintliness almost to the point of deathly coldness. Lucio describes him to Isabella as

> a man whose blood
> Is very snow-broth

suggesting that he is both unnaturally cold and devoid of sexual appetite (blood was often taken to be the seat of sexual passion). Lucio later suggests that these impressions are not confined to himself when he tells the Duke:

> Some report a sea-maid spawned him; some, that he was begot between two stock-fishes. But it is certain that when he makes water, his urine is congealed ice; that I know to be true.

But the Duke is a shrewder judge of character than Lucio, and his description of Angelo as a man who

> scarce confesses
> That his blood flows

indicates that he suspects that Angelo's 'blood' *does* flow and that appearances might be deceptive. This suspicion is expressed more ominously as he adds

> Hence we shall see,
> If power change purpose, what our seemers be.

Angelo is not in his own eyes a 'seemer' and until he meets Isabella he is quite unaware of his hidden sensuality. An Elizabethan audience might have regarded Angelo as a typical Puritan (see *Commentary* 12); to present-day psychologists he could be taken as a classic case-study in sexual repression. Nineteen years spent living in a town where lust and prostitution have been given free rein have made him so disgusted with man's sexual instincts that he has refused to acknowledge their existence within himself.

Modern psychology has discovered that repressed sexual desire does not remain dormant within us and often finds expression in vehemently condemning or attacking the sexual activities of others. This was a truth fully realized by Shakespeare. He expressed it most clearly and powerfully in *King Lear* when the mad king, in a state of almost divine rapture, sees through the injustices which accompany social order and, among a series of revelations, denounces the punishment of a whore:

> Thou rascal beadle, hold thy bloody hand!
> Why dost thou lash that whore? Strip thine own back;
> Thou hotly lust'st to use her in that kind
> For which thou whipp'st her.

No single image in *Measure for Measure* presents the connection between sexual drive and its castigation with such clarity, but it is hinted at throughout the play that the 'sense' which leads Angelo to persecute sexual offenders so relentlessly is not 'reason' but repressed 'sensuality'.

Like all Shakespeare's great creations Angelo reveals his psychological make-up in his own speech. That he delights in hunting down the guilty is made clear in a striking analogy which he uses in justifying to Escalus his zeal in convicting Claudio. He says:

> The jewel that we find, we stoop and take't,
> Because we see it; but what we do not see,
> We tread upon, and never think of it.

To compare a sinner to a jewel is in itself remarkable. Combined with the words 'stoop', which suggests a furtive, underhand action, and 'take', which can have a sexual meaning, the image prefigures Angelo's discovery of Isabella and his dishonourable endeavour to seduce her. This latent sexual significance becomes more clear if we know that the word 'jewel' was sometimes used by Shakespeare as a symbol of 'chastity', an association later reinforced when Angelo tells Isabella that to save Claudio's life she must lay down for him 'the treasures' of her body: i.e. exchange one jewel, Claudio, for another, her virginity.

Angelo and Isabella

The intimation that Isabella will bring out in Angelo the sensuality which he has hitherto been able to 'tread upon' and 'never think of' is given in the scene where Claudio asks Lucio to visit Isabella and implore her to intercede for him with Angelo. His words are:

> bid herself assay him:
> I have great hope in that. For in her youth
> There is a prone and speechless dialect,
> Such as move men.

'Assay' means both 'try' and 'test' and in effect Isabella's first visit to Angelo tests his virtue and she succeeds, without realizing, in 'moving' the blood whose flow he had scarcely acknowledged. The confrontations between the two are made even more dramatic by the fact that she too is being tested. It is no accident that Angelo's servant announces her as

> a very virtuous maid,
> And to be shortly of a sisterhood.

Superficially 'of a sisterhood' means belonging to an order of nuns, but the phrase is ironic in that it also indicates that Isabella's relationship to her brother is to be tested: is her affection for him strong and true?

Isabella comes through the test of her first encounter with Angelo with distinction. Spurred on by Lucio she transforms her 'prone and speechless dialect' into a passionate plea for mercy; mercy not only for her brother, but for all mankind. She turns on Angelo and, echoing Escalus's former words, she tells him:

Go to your bosom,
Knock there, and ask your heart what it doth know
That's like my brother's fault.

The combination of her purity and passion succeed in stirring Angelo
in a way no harlot could. It is not only her words which make him
realize that he is as prone to lust as Claudio: it is herself. At this moment,
when by looking into his heart he might be able to find the grace within
himself to pardon Claudio, Isabella, unaware of the turmoil she has
effected, almost playfully says

Hark how I'll bribe you: good my lord, turn back.

She means, as she goes on to say, that she will pray for his soul, but
Angelo echoes her words 'How? Bribe me?' and already within his
tortured mind the plan is forming to offer her brother's life in exchange
for her virginity.

Isabella has unwittingly been the key to Angelo's repressed self,
but once unlocked his sensuality still cannot find a natural outlet.
It is as though it has become putrid during the long period that he has
denied its existence. In the soliloquy which follows Isabella's departure
he is tormented by images of corruption. He sees the cold, pure novice
as a temple and his lust as a desire to destroy the temple and to pollute
its site:

Having waste ground enough,
Shall we desire to raze the sanctuary,
And pitch our evils there?

Powerful though his sense of self-disgust is, his lust for her is stronger.
When she returns, although he has spent the interim in an attempt at
prayer, he has determined to seduce her.

Angelo has been tested and broken. To Isabella he becomes 'the
devil'; but for the audience the struggle which precedes his fall and his
eventual acknowledgment, 'Blood, thou art blood' makes possible a
flow of sympathy towards him which was impossible when he was an
'angel'.

For Isabella the real test is to come in their next encounter. She is unknowingly in a terrible predicament, for she has come to argue the venial nature of the very sin which Angelo will ask her to commit to save her brother's life. Innocently she announces:

I am come to know your pleasure

and in his aside Angelo takes up the sexual meaning of the word. He poses as an inquisitor and tells Isabella that to pardon a man who has sinfully *made* life would be the equivalent of pardoning a murderer who has sinfully *taken* life. The tension within him is extreme. He is still revolted by the idea of sex, but his initial denunciation of 'These filthy vices' gives way to a succession of prurient images which at one and the same time express his revulsion and his desire. He describes Claudio's sin as an act of 'saucy sweetness' and proceeds to ask Isabella whether, to save her brother from the law, she would give up her body

to such sweet uncleanness
As she that he hath stain'd.

Isabella evades the question in her answer: 'I had rather give my body than my soul.'

In the debate which follows, Angelo leads her step by step into a trap. He is now pursuing virtue with the same relentlessness with which he formerly hunted down vice. The scene is full of dramatic irony, for every comment made by Angelo has a significance for himself and the audience of which Isabella is quite unaware. He asks her if there might not be

a charity in sin
To save this brother's life?

and Isabella, assuming that the sin in question would be, not her own in surrendering to Angelo, but Angelo's in going against his conscience in pardoning Claudio, answers:

Please you to do't,
I'll take it as a peril to my soul,
It is no sin at all, but charity.

Next Angelo asks her whether a sin committed by herself would be of equal charity but Isabella again misunderstands him, thinking that he is referring to the sin of pleading for her brother. Her naïvety seems, to Angelo, to be crafty evasion and he is forced to ask her directly what she would do if told that the only way to save Claudio's life would be to lay down her chastity to someone who could reverse the law. Isabella's answer is now unambiguous. She would prefer death to dishonour, whether that death be her own or her brother's.

Isabella

Isabella's decision is perhaps the most controversial ever made by one of Shakespeare's characters. It is a decision for which both she and Shakespeare have been severely criticized, since it is often assumed that in regarding her chastity as more important than her brother's life she had the whole-hearted approval of her creator. It is of interest to note that in the source play, *Promos and Cassandra* (see *Commentary* 1), Cassandra eventually yields to the judge, Promos. However, we cannot conclude that, because Shakespeare chose to make his heroine cling to her chastity, he was indicating that she was morally superior to Cassandra. It is fruitless to try to isolate Shakespeare's own attitudes from among the many which he presents to us. Isabella is a much more real and interesting character than Cassandra and any suspicion we may have that she is meant to be a faultless heroine should be removed on examining her reaction to Claudio's request that he might live. We have every reason to sympathize with Isabella in her predicament. (She is young, she is totally ignorant of the ways of the world and she is about to dedicate herself to an ideal of chastity.) But it is quite clear that the vehemence of her response stems from the weakness of inexperience rather than from the strength of virtue. The girl who, according to her brother, has 'prosperous art when she will play with reason and discourse', becomes hysterical, and the voice, which had in an earlier scene sounded out like a clarion in its plea for mercy, is now harsh and out of tune as she turns savagely on her brother:

> O, you beast!
> O faithless coward! O dishonest wretch!
> Wilt thou be made a man out of my vice?

Is't not a kind of incest, to take life
From thine own sister's shame? What should I think?
Heaven shield my mother play'd my father fair:
For such a warped slip of wilderness
Ne'er issued from his blood. Take my defiance!
Die, perish! Might but my bending down
Reprieve thee from thy fate, it should proceed.
I'll pray a thousand prayers for thy death,
No word to save thee.

As a novice Isabella may have come through the test satisfactorily: as Claudio's sister she has failed. Whereas Angelo's fall and the genuine inner conflict which precede it make him a much more sympathetic character, Isabella's hysterical and cruel speech to Claudio tends to produce alienation.

Isabella is not intended to be an ideal creation. Although she is treated by both Shakespeare and the Duke with far greater sympathy than is Angelo, she is in some ways very like him. Both are cold. Both are conscious practitioners of virtue. However, whereas Angelo's reformatory zeal is tinged with sadism, Isabella's repressed sexuality is revealed in yearnings which are masochistic. She is about to enter the nunnery to find not only an escape from sin but also a punishment for it. She finds fault with the privileges given to the nuns, not because they are too narrow, but because she desires 'a more strict restraint'. Her psychological inner tension is most apparent when she tells Angelo that she would choose death before dishonour:

were I under the terms of death,
Th' impression of keen whips I'd wear as rubies,
And strip myself to death as to a bed
That longing have been sick for, ere I'd yield
My body up to shame.

Isabella means to say that rather than yield her body up to shame she would suffer death preceded by terrible pain. Yet, she fails to suggest that whipping would be painful to her; rather that she would delight in it. The word 'rubies' which she uses to describe the physical signs of

her suffering, echoes the 'jewel' image with which Angelo uncon-
sciously revealed his delight in discovering a sinner. The masochistic
significance of whipping is enforced in these lines by the use of the
word 'keen', which could mean both 'sharp' and 'sexually eager', and
by the way in which the personification of death changes midway
through the image from a beadle who is beating her to a bed for which
she longs. Moreover, Isabella's is a 'sick' longing, suggesting not so
much the desire of a girl for her lover, as the craving of a woman who
is pregnant. In choosing the seclusion of the nunnery Isabella will be
denying herself the natural fulfilment of child-bearing and the nearest
equivalent which she can experience is a yearning for fulfilment in
death.

Isabella and Lucio

The limitations of life in the nunnery are brought into dramatic
focus when Isabella is visited there by Lucio. Francisca, a nun, has
just informed Isabella of one of the rules which she will soon have to
obey:

> When you have vow'd, you must not speak with men
> But in the presence of the prioress:
> Then, if you speak, you must not show your face;
> Or if you show your face, you must not speak.

The regulation is ridiculously artificial; the rhythm of the lines
intentionally flat. Life in the nunnery may be tranquil and ordered,
but it will also be monotonous and sterile. Then Lucio bursts in and,
in contrast to the lifelessness of Francisca, his rude vigour seems like
life itself. His tone, so often scurrilous, is modified by the presence of
Isabella, and the account which he gives of her brother's love-making is
in the most lyrical language of the play:

> Your brother and his lover have embraced;
> As those that feed grow full, as blossoming time
> That from the seedness the bare fallow brings
> To teeming foison, even so her plenteous womb
> Expresseth his full tilth and husbandry.

For a moment we are able to forget Vienna where sex and disease have until now seemed synonymous. Claudio's love for Julietta is expressed in images of the countryside where increase is natural and wholesome. It is right that Lucio, the man most corrupted by Vienna, should deliver these lines. For Vienna, though squalid, has a fecundity similar to the natural fruitfulness embodied in the speech. Not only Julietta's womb is 'plenteous'; the 'tilth and husbandry' of Elbow is manifested in the womb of his wife who, according to Pompey, enters the brothel 'great-bellied and longing for prunes'; and the brothels themselves can create life, as is witnessed by the child of Mistress Kate Keepdown, fathered by Lucio himself.

In choosing to enter the nunnery, Isabella may be dedicating her virtue to Heaven, but she will be ignoring Nature and, in the words of the Duke:

> Nature never lends
> The smallest scruple of her excellence
> But, like a thrifty goddess, she determines
> Herself the glory of a creditor,
> Both thanks and use.

Lucio

Lucio is described in the *dramatis personae* as a 'fantastic', a term which indicates that his costume and behaviour should be very affected. Every age has its Lucios. Perhaps the nearest contemporary equivalent would be a King's Road Dandy. In the play he is the chief advocate of liberty, especially in sexual matters. In a way he resembles the rat in the lines by Claudio quoted earlier but, unlike Claudio, he accepts his animality with relish. At first our sympathy is completely won over by him. His attitude is refreshing in contrast to the asceticism of Isabella and Angelo, and his is the voice of freedom crying out against tyranny and injustice. He never completely loses our sympathy since he retains an irrepressible vitality and he is always the focal point of humour in the play. However, we are gradually made to realize that for Lucio 'too much liberty' has led to self-indulgence and a complete lack of any sort of self-discipline or moral responsibility. This lack of moral responsibility is at times very engaging. We laugh heartily when he regales 'the Friar' with tales about the Duke's own sexual liberty, imaginatively constructing an image of a 'fantastical Duke of dark corners' which is really a projection of his own 'fantastic' self. Laughter would not have blinded an Elizabethan audience to the fact that Lucio is guilty of slandering a prince, a crime punishable by death, and that when in the final scene he turns on his former 'friend' and accuses him of the self-same slanders, the accusation could have cost 'the Friar' his life. Lack of loyalty is characteristic of Lucio's other personal relationships with the single exception of his initial loyalty to Claudio. Pompey, under arrest, describes him as, 'a gentleman, and a friend', yet Lucio refuses to pay his bail and instead mocks him in his predicament. Soon afterwards Mistress Overdone provides the most damning indictment of him. Although she has looked after his child for over a year, she is arrested as a result of Lucio's informing against her.

Lucio is symptomatic of the general licence plaguing Vienna and his lack of self-discipline shows the need for some sort of state Authority.

THE PROBLEM OF AUTHORITY

That the licence in Vienna is general, and not confined to sexual excess, is made clear in a number of slightly grotesque images of social disorder which run through the play. The Duke tells Friar Thomas:

> Liberty plucks Justice by the nose,
> The baby beats the nurse, and quite athwart
> Goes all decorum.

To the Elizabethans the word 'decorum' meant far more than 'propriety in social relationships'. It was a quality essential not only to social order but also to universal order, as Ulysses stresses in *Troilus and Cressida* when he points out:

> The heavens themselves, the planets and this centre
> Observe degree, priority and place.

The Elizabethans were encouraged by both Church and State to believe that without 'decorum' there must be chaos, and that a prerequisite of decorum on earth was a strong central state authority. They were taught that the King was God's deputy and ruled over his subjects with the same authority that God ruled over the universe. Similarly, in exercising the authority of a king, magistrates (and other deputies) were indirectly wielding a power derived from Heaven. There need therefore be no sarcasm intended by Claudio when he speaks of Angelo as 'the demi-god Authority'.

The belief in the divine authority of kings was championed by Shakespeare in his history plays which show how England was torn by civil war following the usurpation of the throne by Bolingbroke—later crowned as Henry IV. However, by the time that Shakespeare wrote *Measure for Measure* he had started to question the notion that all authority was divine and in the play we are given a frightening glimpse of what may happen when a man with absolute power makes a god of Authority itself. The result is a foretaste of a modern phenomenon, the one-party state, and serves to exemplify Acton's saying—'All power tends to corrupt and absolute power corrupts absolutely.' Abuse of power in the hands of a self-interested tyrant need not be as frightening as power in the hands of an idealist whose idealism is divorced from the realities of human nature.

Human Nature and the Law

Once in power Angelo is confident that the disorder in Vienna can be ended by an immediate and rigid enforcement of those 'strict statutes and most biting laws' which have for so long been neglected. 'We must not make a scarecrow of the law,' he tells Escalus shortly after their appointment. However, he intends the law to perform the same function as a scarecrow: to terrify would-be offenders. By executing Claudio he is doing more than just punishing a sexual offence; by making a grim example of one offender he is hoping to bring an end to all future offences. Escalus, realizing that Claudio's sentence is far too severe, argues that the law should be used to promote cure and not as an instrument of terror and destruction.

Significantly, before appointing Angelo as his deputy, the Duke praised Escalus not only for his knowledge of the law but also for his knowledge of 'the nature' of the people. Angelo is completely lacking in this knowledge and the cold order which he intends as a replacement for the chaos and corruption in Vienna fails to take into account some fundamental truths about mankind: truths which through his seclusion and repression have not reached him. We are reminded of these truths and of the limitations of human law when the discussion between Angelo and Escalus is interrupted by the entry of Elbow, who has arrested Froth and Pompey.

Elbow says 'I do lean upon justice, sir', but he habitually says the opposite of what he means and he may well mean 'Justice leans upon me'. It is immediately clear that, though Elbow's reformatory zeal matches Angelo's, Angelo's ideal state will be a practical impossibility if the law is to be enforced by officers as brainless and inept as Elbow. Although Elbow has blundered on some genuine 'sexual offenders' Angelo listens to his muddled accusations and to Pompey's wily evasions for a short while and then departs leaving Escalus to slowly unravel the truth. Angelo's impatient departure reveals that he is concerned only with the theory of justice and not with its practice. Had he remained he could have learned a great deal from both Escalus and Pompey.

In marked contrast to Angelo's callously abrupt and autocratic manner Escalus conducts the 'trial' of Froth and Pompey with a combination of relaxed good humour and efficiency. He treats Elbow with considerable tact but takes steps to ensure that he will not remain in office. He sees at once that Pompey is 'a bawd' but he lets him off with a warning. Pompey, given this opportunity to reform, decides that he will remain faithful to his 'trade'. But Escalus's tolerance does not prove to be disastrous since he is soon arrested again.

Pompey is a representative of a social group whose welfare Angelo completely ignores. He is 'a bawd', but he is also, in his own words: 'A poor fellow that would live.' He is a 'sinner' not through choice but through necessity and he has a knowledge of human nature far superior to Angelo's. When Escalus tells him that it is the state's intention to do away with prostitution, he answers:

Does your worship mean to geld and splay all the youth of the city?

'Geld' and 'splay' are words normally used for the castration of male and female animals, and the answer aptly reminds the audience that mankind, though often angelic in aspiration, is bestial in body and that no amount of legislation implemented by 'heading' and 'hanging' can alter this fact. Pompey repeatedly reminds us of the limitations of the law which Angelo would like to regard as infallible. When Escalus asks him if being a bawd is 'a lawful trade', Pompey replies, 'If the law would allow it, sir', a reply which we are to remember when in a later scene he agrees to become the hangman's assistant and tells the Provost:

> Sir, I have been an unlawful bawd time out of mind, but yet I will be content to be a lawful hangman.

We are left to ponder the incongruity of a morality which forbids a man to live by prostitution but will pay him to execute his fellows.

Justice and Mercy

If it is Pompey's function to remind the audience of the limitations of law on earth, it is Isabella who stresses its limitations before Heaven. In administering the law, kings and magistrates, as the deputies of God, had the difficult task of balancing Justice and Mercy. Before delegating his authority to Angelo the Duke tells him to let 'mortality and mercy in Vienna' live in his 'tongue and heart'. Angelo's heart is as stone and he is unconcerned about mercy until he is visited by Isabella. The debate which follows might be likened to a scene in a morality play where abstract figures of Justice and Mercy debate the fate of Everyman (see pp. 32–4). However, in the hands of Shakespeare the scene is intensely dramatic since the roles of Justice and Mercy are quite consistent with the personalities of Angelo and Isabella. She tells him that the outward signs of Authority—the crown, the sword, the truncheon and the robe—are less becoming than its invisible accompaniment—Mercy. In a passionate yet controlled speech she reminds him that, since he too is mortal, he is prone to human frailty and may eventually have to answer to a justice higher than earthly justice:

> How would you be,
> If He, which is the top of judgement, should
> But judge you as you are? O, think on that,
> And mercy then will breathe within your lips,

Like man new made.

But Angelo coldly defends the sentence he has passed by claiming that the law is absolute:

It is the law, not I, condemn your brother.

He claims that by rigidly enforcing the law he is really showing pity:

I show it most of all when I show justice;
For then I pity those I do not know.

This is a familiar cry of the revolutionary reformer who advocates violence and destruction now so that the world will be a better place for people yet unborn. But Angelo's claim that he pities those he does not know is really a cover for his complete inability to pity those he does know. His cold self-assurance, and the inhumanity which accompanies it, so enrage Isabella that she bursts into a vehement and scornful attack on the pomposity of all men who wield authority. God, she says, uses his power for a fit purpose; he reserves his thunder-bolts to split mighty oaks, not insignificant small plants,

but man, proud man,
Dressed in a little brief authority,
Most ignorant of what he's most assured—
His glassy essence—like an angry ape
Plays such fantastic tricks before high heaven
As makes the angels weep; who, with our spleens,
Would all themselves laugh mortal.

Her passionate scorn strikes home at Angelo. His besetting sin is pride; the term of his authority is likely to be brief. Notwithstanding his apparent saintliness his reformatory zeal is essentially worldly. He has shown himself to be ignorant of his soul, his 'glassy essence', which is his true link with the angels, and in his endeavour to fashion an ideal state on earth he has achieved merely a worldly superiority which places him as a superior animal: a dressed-up ape, ludicrous to his fellow mortals and sadly ridiculous to the angels whom he endeavours to imitate. The grotesque images of social disorder are now balanced

24

by this grotesque image of man in authority.

The rightness of Isabella's passion must win the sympathy of the audience. But it is characteristic of her that just as her plea for Claudio becomes a plea for Everyman so her denouncement of Angelo becomes a dismissal of all human authority. As such it is a tragically inadequate answer to the problem and could only have come from one who, like Isabella, has renounced this life and is eager for the life to come.

THE PROBLEM OF MORTALITY

The problem of Authority is central to *Measure for Measure* and the reconciliation of Justice and Mercy is a major concern of the final act of the play. However, Isabella and Angelo debate the claims of Justice and Mercy at a highly abstract level and, for this final scene to be dramatically effective, it is necessary that the audience should have considered the concrete significance of the two concepts as they relate to Claudio, for whom mercy will mean life, and justice death. Through Claudio's predicament Shakespeare explores a variety of attitudes to death which drastically affect the actions of several of the characters.

The Duke and Barnardine

When the Duke visits Claudio in the condemned cell he preaches to him a philosophy which is deeply pessimistic. He tells him to

Be absolute for death

but he does not reassure him, as might be expected, of an eternal life to follow. Instead he stresses with great eloquence the pain and uncertainty of life and the certainty that death must eventually come. He tells Claudio to regard death as a great leveller which will release him from the disease of life just as sleep releases us from the pain of wakefulness. The Duke's speech is one of the most compelling in the play and it is impossible not to respond to the hypnotic effect of its rhythmic, repetitive cadences, and to the sublimity of its expression in lines like:

> Thou has nor youth nor age,
> But, as it were, an after-dinner's sleep,
> Dreaming on both.

It is great poetry, but as a philosophy it is acceptable only to a man in a condemned cell. It expresses, in fact, the attitude to life of Barnadine who has been in the condemned cell for nine years:

> A man that apprehends death no more dreadfully but as a drunken sleep; careless, reckless, and fearless of what's past, present, or to come; insensible of mortality, and desperately mortal.

When later confronted with Barnardine, the Duke passes judgment on him as 'Unfit to live or die' and in so doing implicitly condemns the philosophy which he had earlier preached to Claudio. Claudio, however, is grateful for the comfort it provides him and accepts his sentence with stoicism until Isabella reveals to him that he may yet live.

Isabella and Claudio

Isabella endeavours to live according to the principle that life on earth is merely a preparation for the life to come. She regards man's soul, his 'glassy essence', as far more important than his body which, ape-like, must live out its brief yet tedious spell on earth before its soul is made immortal. She herself welcomes the idea of death and her attitude is always apparent. When, for example, she hears of Angelo's treatment of Mariana she immediately says, 'what a merit were it in death to take this poor maid from the world'. Significantly, when Lucio visits her in the nunnery he mockingly pretends that she is dead already, calling her 'a thing enskied and sainted' and 'an immortal spirit'. Since Isabella regards dying as being born forever, she is ill-equipped to plead for Claudio's life and, when she is presented with the alternative of either yielding to Angelo or letting her brother die, she can rationalize it in terms of allowing him 'six or seven winters' in exchange for the immortality of both their souls.

Isabella comes to Claudio not to save him but in the hope that he will save both herself and the family honour by taking her decision upon himself. She is terrified that Claudio may not regard 'perpetual honour' as preferable to a longer life and, instead of telling him openly of Angelo's offer, she speaks to him in language which is as abstract and evasive as was Angelo's in the previous scene where he had attempted to seduce her. Isabella can only think of one reason why men fear death: the physical pain of dying. She tries to reassure Claudio that this pain will be less than he has imagined. She tells him:

> The sense of death is most in apprehension;
> And the poor beetle that we tread upon,
> In corporal sufferance finds a pang as great
> As when a giant dies.

But for Claudio the 'sense of death' is something more than 'corporal sufferance' and, as he gradually realizes that there is yet hope of life, his stoicism falters and he allows his mind to ponder on the awesome-ness of death. His stream of consciousness is expressed in a dream-like speech in which he vividly imagines the horrors of purgatory and hell:

> Ay, but to die, and go we know not where;
> To lie in cold obstruction and to rot;
> This sensible warm motion to become
> A kneaded clod; and the delighted spirit
> To bathe in fiery floods, or to reside
> In thrilling region of thick-ribbed ice;
> To be imprison'd in the viewless winds
> And blown with restless violence round about
> The pendent world; or to be worse than worst
> Of those that lawless and incertain thought
> Imagine howling; 'tis too horrible.
> The weariest and most loathèd worldly life
> That age, ache, penury, and imprisonment
> Can lay on nature is a paradise
> To what we fear of death.

Isabella had hoped that once aware of her predicament Claudio would heroically choose to die. But Claudio is not a 'hero'; he is an Every-man-figure fraught with human weakness and, now that he has imagined fully what it might be like to die, he turns to Isabella with the plea, 'Sweet sister, let me live'. Faced with the responsibility of making the decision herself, the tension within Isabella breaks and she gives vent to her savage reply which culminates in the lines:

> Mercy to thee would prove itself a bawd;
> 'Tis best that thou diest quickly.

Both characters are on the threshold of making terrible discoveries about themselves and their relationship. They are caught in a dilemma from which there seems to be no escape and the play is apparently poised for a tragic resolution. But it was not Shakespeare's intention that the play should be a tragedy and, although the threat of death continues through the second half of the play in the physical presence of Abhorson, the executioner, and in the sentences passed on Angelo and Lucio, its psychological reality is gone.

THE PROBLEMS OF MEASURE FOR MEASURE

Measure for Measure has sometimes been criticized because the problems raised in the first half of the play are never satisfactorily resolved. Although it has been convenient to discuss these 'problems' separately, such division is, of course, artificial. The central problem of the play is the relationship between Justice and Mercy. Man's physical nature and the uncertainty of a life hereafter are inescapable facts about the human condition which are related to this problem in that they preclude the possibility of any rigid idealism as an adequate solution. At the start of the play both Angelo and Isabella are extremists and Shakespeare shows that their extremism is the product of ignorance and seclusion. The title of the play is ambiguous, but one meaning of the word 'measure' which throws light on the play's underlying philosophy is 'moderation' or 'temperance'. Had the play been a novel, Shakespeare could have dealt at length with the way in which his characters modified their attitudes as a result of their experiences. He might have described the joyful reunion of Claudio and Juliet, the good works accomplished by Isabella as Duchess of Vienna, and the suffering experienced by Lucio at the hands of Kate Keepdown. The economy of drama allows for no such luxury, and leaves this kind of speculation to the imagination of the audience. In the second half of the play there is a shift from realism to formality. Claudio does not speak again, and it is Angelo who becomes the focal point of dramatic interest.

II

Tragedy and Tragi-comedy

Shakespeare's tragedies are about calamities which end in death. In his great tragedies the calamity is brought about through something in the character of the hero which either leads him to commit an action which destroys him or else prevents him from committing an action which would save him. Before his death the tragic hero achieves a self-knowledge which he had formerly lacked and with it a sounder understanding of life's values.

In writing *Measure for Measure* Shakespeare was experimenting with a form of drama in which the actions of the hero threaten to cause a calamity but the calamity is averted so that he can experience both self-knowledge and forgiveness and can continue living as a wiser and better man. This form of drama (one of several types of tragi-comedy) interested Shakespeare throughout his career as a dramatist and he was to concentrate on it in his last plays. The structure of one of these *The Winter's Tale*, falls like *Measure for Measure* into two parts, and it is illuminating to contrast the transition from tragedy to comedy in the two plays.

Tragi-comedy in The Winter's Tale

In *The Winter's Tale* King Leontes of Sicily wrongly accuses his wife of adultery with his closest friend, King Polixenes of Bohemia. By the time that he realizes that his accusations are unfounded, his insane jealousy has led to the death of his wife and son and to the severance of a life-long friendship. The first half of the play ends with a scene in which his infant daughter, whom he has refused to recognize as his own, is abandoned on the coast of Bohemia but is saved from destruction by a shepherd.

The action of the second half of the play takes place sixteen years later. Leontes has spent these years in a state of penitential suffering.

His daughter, Perdita, has grown up as a shepherdess and is in love with Polixenes's son. The young couple effect a reconciliation between Leontes and Polixenes and the play ends with the miraculous discovery that Leontes' wife is alive.

The emotional intensity of the first half of *The Winter's Tale* is as painful as in any of Shakespeare's tragedies, but it is released through laughter in the scene on the coast of Bohemia. With Leontes' jealous ravings still echoing in our ears we are made to laugh involuntarily when Antigonus, who has the sad task of abandoning Perdita, is pursued off the stage by a bear. Our laughter continues when a clown enters and gives a very muddled and funny account of the sights he has just witnessed: the wreck of the ship which had brought Perdita and the meal which the bear had made on Antigonus. Laughter releases tension, and in the second half of the play the audience can forget Leontes' jealousy and enjoy the pastoral comedy set in a Bohemia which is as mythical as Illyria (unlike the real Bohemia, it has a coastline).

The tragic realism of the first half of *The Winter's Tale* and the romantic artificiality of the second half are separated, therefore, by a time gap of sixteen years, a complete change in locality and the therapy of laughter.

Tragi-comedy in Measure for Measure

As in *The Winter's Tale* the action of *Measure for Measure* falls into two distinct halves. In the first half Angelo's lack of self-knowledge threatens to destroy both himself and Claudio. In the second half, through the intervention of the Duke calamity is averted, Isabella's honour and Claudio's life are saved, Angelo is publicly exposed and forgiven and the play ends, like other romantic comedies, in a set of arranged marriages.

But in *Measure for Measure* the transition from the tragic mood of the first half of the play to the romantic pattern of the second half is not entirely successful. The change comes at the point where the tension of the play has reached a peak and Isabella has turned on Claudio with her defiant and final cry:

> Mercy to thee would prove itself a bawd;
> 'Tis best that thou diest quickly.

The Duke intervenes and, in marked contrast to the passionate interchange which preceded his intervention, he speaks in a flat prose which brings an immediate halt to the tension:

> Vouchsafe a word, young sister, but one word. . . . Might you dispense with your leisure, I would by and by have some speech with you: the satisfaction I would require is likewise your own benefit.

Still talking in this toneless, artificial prose the Duke tells Isabella the story of Mariana, a young woman who had been betrothed to Angelo but had been jilted by him because she had lost her dowry. Isabella readily agrees to arrange a meeting with Angelo and to allow Mariana to take her place in the encounter.

Mariana and the Conventions of Romantic Comedy

The 'dejected Mariana' is a character from the world of romantic comedy. She is the sister of 'Frederick, the great soldier who miscarried at sea' and she lives at a 'moated grange' lamenting the loss of her lover and indulging her grief by listening to sad songs. Her character and situation are, in fact, a fusion of the characters and situations of Orsino and Viola in *Twelfth Night*.

The story of Mariana is intended to bring the tension of the first half of the play to a halt and to prepare the audience for the conventions of romantic comedy which operate through the second half. In a play set in a make-believe world like Illyria, the Forest of Arden or pastoral Bohemia, it is easy to suspend disbelief and to accept improbabilities and impossibilities which further the development of the plot. Many readers of *Measure for Measure*, however, will find the story of Mariana quite insufficient to dispel the realism of Vienna so that they can uncritically accept the 'bed-trick' which enables Angelo to think that he is violating Isabella when he is really sleeping with his own betrothed. Such readers may find the romantic conclusion to the play, with Isabella receiving a marriage proposal from the Duke, totally unsatisfactory as a resolution of the seemingly intractable problems presented in the earlier part of the play. But the romantic conventions which may seem quite unconvincing when the play is studied or read are much easier to accept on the stage. *Measure for Measure* 'acts' well today and must have acted even better before an audience who were familiar with romance conventions both in the plays which they saw acted and in the novels which they read.

Even if we can accept the transition from realism to romance, the device of Mariana might be considered flawed for two reasons. First it results in a marked fall in the quality of the play's language, and although this does effect a break in tension it remains artistically clumsy. Secondly, it involves a severe distortion of two of the characters who had been drawn with such psychological realism in the first half of the play. The audience is asked to believe that the pure and idealistic Isabella would readily accept the Duke's plot and allow Mariana to take her place in the assignation with Angelo and in so doing commit the same offence for which Claudio had been convicted. And, although the discovery that Angelo had contemplated marrying Mariana for her money may enrich the dramatic structure of the play by providing an opportunity to contrast Angelo's prudence with Claudio's 'sinful' recklessness, the details of his affair with Mariana are not in accordance with the strict austerity of his life as it is described by the Duke and other characters. The Elizabethans, however, had a very different conception of 'character' in drama from our own and this should become evident after considering the influence of morality drama on *Measure for Measure*.

Morality Plays

The fifteenth century was the great age of morality drama, but as late as 1570 morality plays remained the most popular form of entertainment at the English court. Their influence on Shakespeare and his contemporaries was considerable.

The central character in a morality play was not an individual but a symbol of humanity as a whole and was given a name like Everyman or Mankind. Other characters included God and his Angels, Lucifer and his Devils, and personifications of a variety of abstractions such as Justice, Mercy, Truth and the Seven Deadly Sins. The cast for the play

Everyman included among its characters, God, Good deeds, Knowledge, Beauty and Strength. Although there was considerable variety in the episodes which made up different morality plays, the pattern of the action was nearly always the same. Mankind set out on his journey through life and, despite the good advice given him by the Virtues, he succumbed easily to the temptations of the Vices. He seemed set on a path towards everlasting perdition but as he approached Death he repented and through the intervention of divine grace his soul was saved. In the oldest of the few extant morality plays, *The Castle of Perseverance*, the final scene takes place after the death of Mankind. Before the throne of God his fate is debated by Justice and Mercy and his soul is only saved after Mercy's plea for its forgiveness has triumphed over Justice's demand for its damnation.

Morality Plays and Measure for Measure

Thematically *Measure for Measure* and the morality plays have obvious similarities. Both stress the frailty of human nature and the inevitability of death, and both have as their central theme the forgiveness of sinful man. Concrete evidence that *Measure for Measure* was influenced by morality drama emerges from a study of the play's characters. Shakespeare had an unparalleled gift for creating character and, in responding to his creations as though they were real human beings, we are likely to neglect the fact that they often have a symbolic function as well. A glance at the names of the characters in *Measure for Measure* will at once reveal this. The names of Elbow ('I do lean upon justice'), Froth, Mistress Overdone and Abhorson (son-of-a-whore) suggest that these characters are types as well as individuals. Angelo's name is a good deal more meaningful than it might at first seem. It tells us not only that he denies that his nature is in part bestial, and that like the coin, the angel, he will be given the stamp of authority, but also that like the fallen angel, Lucifer, his besetting sin is pride and once he has fallen he will take on the role of the devil. Lucio's name might be intended as an abbreviation of Lucifer, or it might mean 'light' in the sense of 'levity'. However, it is his dramatic function rather than his name which links him with the morality drama. He is very similar to 'the Vice' (also called 'Iniquity') a character abounding in vitality, whose words and actions were a source of entertainment to the audience despite the fact that they invariably contributed to the spiritual and physical ruin of frail humanity. Other characters whose roles resemble those of the stock figures from the morality drama are Isabella, who twice takes on the role of Mercy, first pleading for Claudio and then for Angelo, and Claudio himself, who starts out as an Everyman-figure approaching death and is the focal point of the audience's sympathy and identification throughout the first half of the play.

But the character whose actions we are most likely to interpret incorrectly if we completely disregard the non-naturalistic dimension of the play is the Duke Vincentio.

The Character and Actions of the Duke

If judged by the standards of real life the Duke's actions are indefensible. It would be impossible to excuse a headmaster who, having failed to enforce discipline in his school, handed over his authority to his vice-principal and then spied on him disguised as the school chaplain. But, unlike the other main characters, the Duke's actions are not psychologically motivated. Shakespeare has made him less 'real' than Claudio, Isabella and Angelo because he has an important dramatic function to perform: it is he who controls the action and steers the play from tragedy to comedy. All the same, he is more than a mere dramatic device. He has been illuminatingly described as more of a power than a character. This description is based, in part, on Angelo's acknowledgment made on realizing that the Duke has been aware of his deception:

> O my dread lord,
> I should be guiltier than my guiltiness,
> To think I can be undiscernible,
> When I perceive your Grace, like power divine,
> Hath look'd upon my passes.

These lines are central to several fairly recent interpretations of *Measure for Measure* in which the Duke is seen as a Christ-figure moving among his people in an endeavour to save them from their sinful condition. One of these interpretations shows that the play abounds in echoes of

Christ's parables (cf. *Commentary* 4) and compares the action of the play to an inversion of the parable of the Unmerciful Servant (Matthew, xviii). Another interpretation finds in the action parallels of the Incarnation, Second Coming and Last Judgment. If *Measure for Measure* is read in this way as a Christian allegory, Isabella's marriage with the Duke can be conveniently likened to the Nun's marriage with Christ or, more symbolically, to the union of mercy with justice or of innocence with experience.

Undoubtedly *Measure for Measure* is closer to allegory than are any other of Shakespeare's plays and an Elizabethan audience would have been readier to look for hidden meaning than we are today. But it was not Shakespeare's practice to write simple allegory, and though an allegorical interpretation may give added enjoyment to some people it should not obscure the fact that *Measure for Measure's* main preoccupation is with human nature. The Duke may be 'like power divine' and he undoubtedly controls the action of the play but, like Angelo, he is also a man, and as such he is fallible. Were he infallible a good deal of the excitement, the dramatic tension and the humour would be lost completely. Moreover, while the Duke's manipulation of the plot gives the play dramatic coherence, his character as a man provides it with a thematic unity.

The Duke is described by Escalus as 'one that, above all other strifes, contended especially to know himself'. His taking on the disguise of a Friar and moving among the people of Vienna might be interpreted as an endeavour to learn more about the people whom he governs. For it was the function of the ideal ruler to govern his kingdom in the same way that God ruled the universe and the soul of an individual controlled his body. This analogy had its origins in medieval philosophy and is stated as follows by St Thomas Aquinas:

> Therefore let the King recognize that by the terms of the office which he undertakes, he is to be in the kingdom as the soul is in the body and as God is in the universe.

And, just as Angelo requires a knowledge of his animal nature before he can control it, so the Duke requires a knowledge of his subjects before he can prove an effective governor.

As the Duke moves among the occupants of Vienna's brothels and prisons he discovers in them strengths and weaknesses which he could never have detected had he remained in authority. He comments sententiously on all he sees: on Pompey's lack of hypocrisy, on Julietta's penitence, and on the compassion of the Provost. He discovers in Angelo a capacity for evil which even he had not suspected. There are moments when the smug and prolix *sententiae* threaten to become tedious, but the Duke meets one of his subjects who ensures that any tedium must be short lived. This is, of course, Lucio, from whom the Duke is forced to learn, if not more about himself, more about the image of himself which has resulted from his lax administration.

The Duke and Lucio

The Duke's encounters with Lucio take place in a classically comic situation and form the high points of the play's comedy. The audience and the Duke know that 'the Friar' is really the Duke. Lucio assumes that he is a harmless priest and practitioner of a system of outmoded moral values. And extravagantly Lucio proceeds to paint for 'the Friar's' entertainment, a picture of 'the Duke' as an intimate friend of his, a drunken elderly lecher, now too old to perform the sexual act himself but benevolently encouraging its unrestrained practice among his subjects:

Ere he would have hanged a man for the getting a hundred bastards, he would have paid for the nursing a thousand. He had some feeling of the sport; he knew the service; and that instructed him to mercy.

But the joke is by no means only against 'the Friar', for when they next meet Lucio lets slip one example of the Duke's 'mercy' which he is later to regret. Lucio had been in court before him for 'getting a wench with child', but merely by denying that he had done so he had escaped the penalty which would have been imposed: this was not death but, for Lucio a fate far worse, marriage.

Lucio is the only character whom the Duke finds that he cannot entirely forgive. This is not because Lucio has slandered him, but because Lucio is himself incapable of any form of penitence. The Duke's prime object is not to punish sinners but to make them aware of their sinful condition. They must learn to know themselves before they can be forgiven.

Measure for Measure

The Duke's manipulation of the action culminates in the great final scene in which Angelo is first publicly exposed and then forgiven. This scene gives the play a dramatic unity and justifies the rambling short scenes which immediately precede it. We now remember Isabella's warning to Angelo:

> How would you be,
> If He, which is the top of judgement, should
> But judge you as you are?

and Angelo's justification of the sentence which he had passed on Claudio:

> When I, that censure him, do so offend,
> Let mine own judgement pattern out my death.

The roles are now changed. Angelo faces death and Isabella stridently calls for 'justice, justice, justice, justice!' The title of the play suggests that Angelo will be punished as he deserves, and when the Duke as a spokesman of a higher justice announces:

> The very mercy of the law cries out
> Most audible, even from his proper tongue,
> 'An Angelo for Claudio, death for death!'
> Haste still pays haste, and leisure answers leisure;
> Like doth quit like, and Measure still for Measure.

it seems that the play is to be a play of revenge based on the Old Testament philosophy of 'an eye for an eye and a tooth for a tooth'. But this is not the meaning of 'Measure for Measure' which the Duke intends. He is giving Isabella her final test, and she, kept ignorant of the fact that her brother is still alive, is able to perform an act of true compassion. She kneels with Mariana before the Duke and once more makes good use of her ability to 'persuade'. Angelo, believing that he is guilty of murder, would be pleased to die, but with the discovery that Claudio lives he too forgives himself, there is 'a quickening in his eye' and he is a 'man new made'.

The great Shakespearean critic, Samuel Taylor Coleridge, found it impossible to join Isabella in forgiving Angelo and wrote, 'the pardon and marriage of Angelo baffles the strong indignant claim of Justice'.

Coleridge seems to have been less bewildered by the ending of *The Merchant of Venice*, which is in some ways the more disturbing play. Both Shylock, the Jew, and Angelo, the Puritan, would have aroused prejudices in Shakespeare's original audience. There were few Jews living in England, but throughout Europe Jews were associated with usury (a practice condemned by Christians as sinful, yet permitted through economic necessity) and were therefore feared and hated. Puritans were particularly disliked by theatre-loving Elizabethans since they advocated the closing of the theatres. In the plays of Shakespeare's contemporaries Jews and Puritans were stock comic villains.

In *The Merchant of Venice* Shakespeare unexpectedly allows the villain Shylock to reveal to the audience that he is not just 'a devil' in disguise. He turns on the Christians who are taunting him and says:

> I am a Jew. Hath not a Jew eyes? hath not a Jew hands, organs, dimensions, senses, affections, passions? . . . If you prick us, do we not bleed? if you tickle us do we not laugh? if you poison us do we not die? and if you wrong us, shall we not revenge?

But Shylock's humanity is forgotten in the excitement of the trial scene, and the audience are invited to share the vindictive jubilation of the Christian community at his fall. There is, thus, a clash between theme and action. Portia preaches a doctrine of mercy identical to Isabella's yet the mercy which Shylock is given is very 'strained'. Although he agrees to be baptized a Christian, he makes his final exit to the accompaniment of discordant jeering and he remains unforgiven and an alien in a Christian world.

No similar discord mars the end of *Measure for Measure*. It is impossible to sympathize with the cold, autocratic and self-sufficient Angelo of the opening scenes of the play, but once he has struggled with temptation he ceases to be saint or devil and becomes, like Claudio before him, a symbol of poor, weak, erring humanity. In the Duke's own words:

> O, what may man within him hide,
> Though angel on the outward side.

The final test in *Measure for Measure* is not for Isabella or for Angelo, but for the audience. It is easy to forgive Claudio and to be resentful of the puritanical Angelo who will not do so. It is far more difficult to forgive Angelo. Coleridge discovered this but he misinterpreted the play in thinking that the difficulty constituted a flaw. Like the morality plays which preceded it *Measure for Measure* is a play in the form of a dramatized sermon. Its text, as its title suggests, is taken from a famous passage which occurs in the gospels of both St Matthew and St Luke:

> Judge not, that ye be not judged. For with what judgement ye judge, ye shall be judged: and with what measure ye mete, it shall be measured to you again.

In considering the implications of the title it is necessary to consider the whole of this quotation. Perhaps 'Judge not, that ye be not judged', rather than the stern conclusion of the passage, most nearly expresses the central theme of the play.

WILLIAM SHAKESPEARE

A BIOGRAPHICAL NOTE

ALTHOUGH Shakespeare lived during the greatest period of English drama, his was not an age when the art of the dramatist was highly valued: he did nothing to ensure that his plays were carefully printed, and none of his contemporaries attempted to write his biography. We know more about Shakespeare's life than that of any other dramatist of the period, with the exception of Ben Jonson, but almost all that we know has been deduced from official records, which tell us virtually nothing about his private life. However, ever since Shakespeare came to be regarded as a great writer, there has been an abundance of speculation about him. The Restoration pictured him as a fun-loving, irresponsible young man from Stratford, who was later to become a rather dissolute London wit. The Augustans stressed his lack of learning and imagined him as a rude, untutored genius. By the nineteenth century (when Shakespeare had attained universal fame) it was fashionable to believe that his works contained sentiments too noble to have come from an ignorant burgher of Stratford, and attempts were made to prove that they had been written by Sir Francis Bacon (who, it was suggested, was really the son of Queen Elizabeth). In this century other 'Shakespeare claimants' have been put forward including Christopher Marlowe, the Earl of Essex and Queen Elizabeth herself.

The scholarship of the last hundred years has provided the basis for a sounder but less romantic biography. William Shakespeare was christened in Stratford-on-Avon on 26 April 1564. His father was John Shakespeare, a prominent citizen of Stratford who had married Mary Arden, the daughter of a nearby landowner. As the son of well-to-do parents, Shakespeare probably went to the local grammar school, where he would have received a solid grounding in Latin and where he might well have discovered the beginnings of his life-long enthusiasm for Ovid. At the age of eighteen he married Anne Hathaway and some six months later a daughter, Susanna, was born to them. (It has been suggested that, like Claudio and Juliet in *Measure for Measure*, the couple might have been secretly betrothed before their wedding.) On 2 February 1585 a son and daughter, Hamnet and Judith, were christened. Town records show that Shakespeare kept contact with Stratford throughout his London years. He bought the second largest house in the town in 1597, and was buried in Stratford in 1616.

We do not know what happened to Shakespeare between his leaving Stratford and his arrival in London. We do know from an allusion in Robert Greene's *Groatsworth of Wit* that by 1592 he had established a reputation as an actor–playwright. In 1594 he became a member of the newly-formed Chamberlain's Men, destined to become one of the two most successful companies of actors in London.

Elizabethan drama owed much of its greatness to Queen Elizabeth's need to economize. She could not afford to keep her own court actors so she made use of the companies which already existed. She called upon them to provide court entertainment whenever it was required. They were paid for their services, but for the major part of the year they had to live off their earnings from public performances. Thus the best Elizabethan drama was able to satisfy a sophisticated court audience while still appealing to the more varied tastes of those who attended the public theatres. It is probable that Shakespeare wrote most of his plays with both audiences in mind. He remained with the Chamberlain's Men (known under King James I as the King's Men) for the whole of his dramatic career. He must have come to know intimately the strengths and weaknesses of the actors for whom he wrote. The great tragic roles were undoubtedly written for Richard Burbage, who rivalled Edward Alleyn of the Admiral's Men as the greatest tragedian of the age. The leading comic roles in the early plays were written for William Kempe, who had a flair for buffoonery, but when Kempe left the company he was replaced by Robert Armin, a more sophisticated clown for whom the parts of Touchstone, Feste and the fool in *King Lear* were apparently written.

To two of his fellow actors, John Heminge and Henry Condell, we are indebted for the first collected edition of Shakespeare's plays—the First Folio, published in 1623, seven years after his death. It contained thirty-six plays (the accepted canon, excluding *Pericles*). Of these, nineteen had already been published separately in quarto.

It is impossible to state with certainty the exact order in which Shakespeare's plays were written. The following table may help to illustrate his development as an artist. The dating is approximate.

Comedies	Histories	Tragedies
The Comedy of Errors	Henry VI, Parts	Titus Andronicus
The Taming of the Shrew	1, 2 and 3	
The Two Gentlemen of Verona	Richard III	

1593 A plague epidemic between June 1592 and May 1594 resulted in the closing of the theatres for much of the time. It was probably during this period that Shakespeare wrote his two narrative poems, *Venus and Adonis* and the *Rape of Lucrece*.

Love's Labour's Lost	King John	
A Midsummer Night's Dream	Richard II	Romeo and Juliet
The Merchant of Venice	Henry IV,	
Much Ado About Nothing	Parts 1 and 2	
The Merry Wives of Windsor	Henry V	Julius Caesar
As You Like It		
Twelfth Night		
1600 All's Well That Ends Well		Hamlet
Troilus and Cressida		Othello
Measure for Measure		King Lear
		Macbeth
		Antony and
		Cleopatra
		Coriolanus
		Timon of Athens
1608 Pericles		
Cymbeline		
The Winter's Tale		
The Tempest	Henry VIII	
1613		

(It seems likely that most of Shakespeare's *Sonnets* were written between 1592 and 1598, but some may be later.)

42

MEASURE FOR MEASURE

by

WILLIAM SHAKESPEARE

DRAMATIS PERSONAE

VINCENTIO, *Duke of Vienna*
ANGELO, *his Deputy*
ESCALUS, *an ancient Lord*
CLAUDIO, *a young gentleman*
LUCIO, *a fantastic*
PROVOST
FRIAR THOMAS
FRIAR PETER
ELBOW, *a simple constable*
FROTH, *a foolish gentleman*
POMPEY, *servant to Mistress Overdone*
ABHORSON, *an executioner*
BARNARDINE, *a dissolute prisoner*
VARRIUS, *a nobleman*
A JUSTICE
Two gentlemen

ISABELLA, *sister to Claudio*
MARIANA, *betrothed to Angelo*
JULIET, *beloved of Claudio*
FRANCISCA, *a nun*
MISTRESS OVERDONE, *a bawd*
*Lords, Officers, Citizens, Boy, Messenger and
Servants*

SCENE: *Vienna*

ACT I

SCENE I. *Vienna*

Enter DUKE, ESCALUS, Lords *and* Attendants

Duke	Escalus.
Escalus	My lord.
Duke	Of government the properties to unfold
	Would seem in me t'affect speech and discourse,
	Since I am put to know that your own science 5
	Exceeds, in that, the lists of all advice
	My strength can give you. Then no more remains,
	But that, to your sufficiency, [
	] as your worth is able,
	And let them work. The nature of our people, 10
	Our city's institutions, and the terms
	For common justice, you're as pregnant in
	As art and practice hath enriched any
	That we remember. There is our commission,
	From which we would not have you warp. Call hither, 15
	I say, bid come before us Angelo.
	(*Exit an Attendant*

Vienna: See *Commentary 3*, 'Scene Localities'.

3–4. *Of government . . . discourse:* It would be an affectation were I to talk at length about the essential qualities of government.

5. *put:* made. *science:* knowledge.

6. *lists:* limits.

7. *strength:* authority.

7–10. *Then . . . work:* Most editors agree that a line is missing here. (See *Commentary 2*, 'The Text of *Measure for Measure*'.) The Duke is apparently telling Escalus to combine with his own ability the authority which is being given to him.

8. *sufficiency:* ability.

10–14. *The nature . . . remember:* You have learned, through theory and practice, as much about the temperament of our people, the political and social customs of the city and the conditions for administering justice, as anyone that I can remember.

12. *pregnant:* resourceful.

15. *warp:* deviate.

What figure of us think you he will bear?
For you must know, we have with special soul
Elected him our absence to supply;
Lent him our terror, dress'd him with our love,   20
And given his deputation all the organs
Of our own power: what think you of it?

Escalus If any in Vienna be of worth
To undergo such ample grace and honour,
It is Lord Angelo.

Duke   Look where he comes.   25

Enter ANGELO

Angelo Always obedient to your Grace's will,
I come to know your pleasure.

Duke   Angelo:
There is a kind of character in thy life
That to th' observer doth thy history
Fully unfold. Thyself and thy belongings   30
Are not thine own so proper as to waste
Thyself upon thy virtues, they on thee.
Heaven doth with us as we with torches do,
Not light them for themselves; for if our virtues
Did not go forth of us, 'twere all alike   35
As if we had them not. Spirits are not finely
      touch'd
But to fine issues; nor Nature never lends

17. *What figure . . . bear?:* How will he represent me? (See also *Commentary 5*, 'Coining Images'.)
18. *special soul:* particularly careful thought.
20. *terror:* the power of life and death.   *dress'd him with our love:* endowed him with the love which subjects should naturally feel for their ruler.
21. *deputation:* office as deputy.   *organs:* instruments.
24. *undergo:* bear the weight of.
28. *character:* distinctive quality.
29. *history:* life story.
30-2. *Thyself . . . on thee:* Neither yourself nor your virtues are so fully your own that you can waste them on each other.
33-41. *Heaven . . . Both thanks and use:* See *Commentary 4*, 'The Parable of the Talents'.
36-7. *Spirits . . . fine issues:* i.e. moral excellence should manifest itself actively.

46

The smallest scruple of her excellence
But, like a thrifty goddess, she determines
Herself the glory of a creditor,   40
Both thanks and use. But I do bend my speech
To one that can my part in him advertise;
Hold therefore, Angelo:
In our remove be thou at full ourself;
Mortality and mercy in Vienna   45
Live in thy tongue and heart. Old Escalus,
Though first in question, is thy secondary.
Take thy commission.

Angelo   Now, good my lord,
Let there be some more test made of my metal,
Before so noble and so great a figure   50
Be stamp'd upon it.

Duke   No more evasion:
We have with a leaven'd and prepared choice
Proceeded to you; therefore take your honours.
Our haste from hence is of so quick condition
That it prefers itself, and leaves unquestion'd   55
Matters of needful value. We shall write to you,
As time and our concernings shall importune,
How it goes with us; and do look to know
What doth befall you here. So, fare you well.

41. *bend:* direct.
42. *To one . . . advertise:* To someone who could himself demonstrate how to rule.
43. *Hold:* this might mark the moment when the Duke hands the commission to Angelo, or it might be a warning to him to hold on to the qualities which he seems to have.
44. *remove:* absence.
45. *Mortality and mercy:* the power of life and death.
47. *in question:* to be consulted.
40–51. *Let there be . . . stamp'd upon it:* See *Commentary* 5, 'Coining Images'.
49. *metal:* there is a pun on 'mettle', meaning 'quality' or 'disposition'.
52. *leaven'd and prepared choice:* choice resulting from mature thought and preparation.
54–6. *Our haste . . . value:* the reason for my departure is so urgent that it takes precedence over other important matters, leaving them unattended.
57. *concernings:* affairs. *importune:* urge.
58. *look:* expect.

	To th'hopeful execution do I leave you	60
	Of your commissions.	

Angelo   Yet give leave, my lord,
That we may bring you something on the way.

Duke   My haste may not admit it;
Nor need you, on mine honour, have to do
With any scruple. Your scope is as mine own,   65
So to enforce or qualify the laws
As to your soul seems good. Give me your hand:
I'll privily away. I love the people,
But do not like to stage me to their eyes:
Though it do well, I do not relish well   70
Their loud applause and Aves vehement;
Nor do I think the man of safe discretion
That does affect it. Once more, fare you well.

Angelo   The heavens give safety to your purposes!

Escalus   Lead forth and bring you back in happiness!   75

Duke   I thank you. Fare you well.   (Exit

Escalus   I shall desire you, sir, to give me leave
To have free speech with you; and it concerns me
To look into the bottom of my place:
A power I have, but of what strength and nature   80
I am not yet instructed.

Angelo   'Tis so with me. Let us withdraw together,
And we may soon our satisfaction have

60. *hopeful:* promising.
62. *bring . . . way:* accompany you on part of your journey.
64–5. *have . . . scruple:* have any doubts (about the Duke's private departure).
65. *scope:* extent of power.
66. *qualify:* alter.
67. *soul:* intelligence.
68. *privily:* privately.
68–73. *I love . . . affect it:* See *Commentary* 6, 'The Duke and King James'.
69. *stage me:* exhibit myself.
70–1. *Though . . . Aves vehement:* Though it is right that they should applaud and cheer their ruler, I do not enjoy it.
73. *affect:* enjoy.
78. *free:* frank.
78–9. *and it . . . place:* and I ought to sound out thoroughly my position.
80. *power:* kind of authority.

Touching that point.

Escalus   I'll wait upon your honour.

                                                    (*Exeunt*

SCENE II. *A Street*

Enter LUCIO *and two other* Gentlemen

Lucio   If the Duke, with the other dukes, come not to
             composition with the King of Hungary, why then
             all the dukes fall upon the King.
1st Gent.   Heaven grant us its peace, but not the King of
             Hungary's!   5
2nd Gent.   Amen.
Lucio   Thou concludest like the sanctimonious pirate,
             that went to sea with the Ten Commandments, but
             scraped one out of the table.
2nd Gent.   'Thou shalt not steal'?   10
Lucio   Ay, that he razed.
1st Gent.   Why, 'twas a commandment to command the
             captain and all the rest from their functions: they
             put forth to steal. There's not a soldier of us all,
             that, in the thanksgiving before meat, do relish 15
             the petition well that prays for peace.
2nd Gent.   I never heard any soldier dislike it.
Lucio   I believe thee; for I think thou never wast where
             grace was said.
2nd Gent.   No? A dozen times at least.   20
1st Gent.   What, in metre?
Lucio   In any proportion or in any language.
1st Gent.   I think, or in any religion.

1–15. See *Commentary 7.*
2. *composition:* political settlement. (See *Commentary 8.*)
2–3. *why then . . . the King:* then (surely) all the Dukes will attack the King.
4. *its:* i.e. Heaven's.
13. *functions:* vocations.
22. *proportion:* metrical or musical rhythm.   *language:* Roman Catholic graces
    were said in Latin.

49

Lucio	Ay, why not? Grace is grace, despite of all controversy: as, for example, thou thyself art a 25 wicked villain, despite of all grace.
1st Gent.	Well, there went but a pair of shears between us.
Lucio	I grant: as there may between the lists and the velvet. Thou art the list.
1st Gent.	And thou the velvet: thou art good velvet; 30 thou'rt a three-piled piece, I warrant thee! I had as lief be a list of an English kersey, as be piled, as thou art piled, for a French velvet. Do I speak feelingly now?
Lucio	I think thou dost; and, indeed, with most painful 35 feeling of thy speech. I will, out of thine own confession, learn to begin thy health; but whilst I live, forget to drink after thee.
1st Gent.	I think I have done myself wrong, have I not?
2nd Gent.	Yes, that thou hast; whether thou art tainted or 40 free.
Lucio	Behold, behold, where Madam Mitigation comes! I have purchased as many diseases under her roof as come to——

24–6. *Grace . . . all grace:* Lucio plays on the double meaning of grace: thanksgiving and the divine favour directed to sinners.

25. *controversy:* argument between religious sects.

27. *there . . . between us:* we were cut from the same cloth, i.e. Lucio is also a wicked villain.

28–29. *the lists and the velvet:* Lucio develops the cloth metaphor, suggesting that the shears cut between the plain edging (*list*) and the true velvet, i.e. that his friend is common and he a fine gentleman.

30–3. *And thou . . . French velvet:* The First Gentleman retaliates by saying that he would rather be a plain healthy Englishman than a fine gentleman suffering from venereal disease. *Three-piled* velvet was particularly soft and rich, but 'pilled' meant bald, loss of hair being one of the consequences thought to have resulted from syphilis, the 'French disease'.

32. *English kersey:* a plain cloth.

34. *feelingly:* to the purpose.

37. *begin thy health:* propose your toast.

38. *forget to drink after thee:* not drink from your cup (through fear of being infected by you).

39. *done myself wrong:* discredited myself.

40. *tainted:* infected.

42. *Madam Mitigation:* Mistress Overdone: so called because her trade 'mitigates' or lessens desire.

2nd Gent.	To what, I pray?	45
Lucio	Judge.	
2nd Gent.	To three thousand dolours a year.	
1st Gent.	Ay, and more.	
Lucio	A French crown more.	
1st Gent.	Thou art always figuring diseases in me; but thou art full of error; I am sound.	50
Lucio	Nay, not, as one would say, healthy; but so sound as things that are hollow: thy bones are hollow; impiety has made a feast of thee.	

Enter MISTRESS OVERDONE

1st Gent.	How now, which of your hips has the most profound sciatica?	55
Mistr. Overdone	Well, well! There's one yonder arrested and carried to prison was worth five thousand of you all.	
2nd Gent.	Who's that, I prithee?	60
Mistr. Overdone	Marry sir, that's Claudio, Signior Claudio.	
1st Gent.	Claudio to prison? 'Tis not so.	
Mistr. Overdone	Nay, but I know 'tis so: I saw him arrested; saw him carried away; and, which is more, within these three days his head to be chopped off.	65
Lucio	But, after all this fooling, I would not have it so. Art thou sure of this?	
Mistr. Overdone	I am too sure of it: and it is for getting Madam Julietta with child.	
Lucio	Believe me, this may be: he promised to meet me two hours since, and he was ever precise in promise-keeping.	70

---

47. *dolours:* a pun on dollars and 'dolours', meaning misfortunes.
49. *A French crown:* a pun on the coin called a crown and the bald head thought to result from 'the French disease'.
55–6. *How now . . . sciatica:* A question probably addressed to Lucio but taken up by Mistress Overdone. (Bawds in Latin comedy frequently suffer from sciatica.)

2nd Gent.	Besides, you know, it draws something near to the speech we had to such a purpose.
1st Gent.	But most of all agreeing with the proclamation. 75
Lucio	Away! Let's go learn the truth of it.

(Exeunt Lucio and Gentlemen

Mistr. Overdone	Thus, what with the war, what with the sweat, what with the gallows, and what with poverty, I am custom-shrunk.

Enter POMPEY

	How now? What's the news with you? 80
Pompey	Yonder man is carried to prison.
Mistr. Overdone	Well! What has he done?
Pompey	A woman.
Mistr. Overdone	But what's his offence?
Pompey	Groping for trouts in a peculiar river. 85
Mistr. Overdone	What? Is there a maid with child by him?
Pompey	No, but there's a woman with maid by him. You have not heard of the proclamation, have you?
Mistr. Overdone	What proclamation, man? 90
Pompey	All houses in the suburbs of Vienna must be plucked down.

73. *something*: somewhat.
75. *the proclamation*: a declaration issued by Angelo announcing the severe measures which he had introduced to bring an end to sexual licence.
77–9. *Thus . . . custom-shrunk*: See *Commentary* 9.
77. *the sweat*: the name given to the outbreak of plague in 1603.
79. *I am custom-shrunk*: my trade has been drastically reduced.
81. *Yonder man*: It has been suggested that Pompey must be referring to someone other than Claudio since Mistress Overdone already knows of his arrest. However, it is more probable that Shakespeare is guilty of an inconsistency here.
82. *done*: this is the first of a series of puns on the sexual meaning of the verb 'to do'.
85. *Groping . . . river*: having sexual intercourse; an image based on 'tickling trout', a way of poaching. Pompey regards Julietta as a 'peculiar' or 'private' river since, unlike Mistress Overdone's girls, she is not available to the general public.
87. *maid*: a name given to the young of certain sorts of fish.
91. *houses*: brothels.

Mistr. Overdone And what shall become of those in the city?

Pompey   They shall stand for seed: they had gone down too,
           but that a wise burgher put in for them.   95

Mistr. Overdone But shall all our houses of resort in the suburbs be
           pulled down?

Pompey   To the ground, mistress.

Mistr. Overdone Why, here's a change indeed in the common-
           wealth! What shall become of me?   100

Pompey   Come; fear not you: good counsellors lack no
           clients: though you change your place, you need
           not change your trade: I'll be your tapster still.
           Courage! There will be pity taken on you: you
           that have worn your eyes almost out in the 105
           service, you will be considered.

Mistr. Overdone What's to do here, Thomas Tapster? Let's with-
           draw.

Pompey   Here comes Signior Claudio, led by the provost
           to prison; and there's Madam Juliet.   110

                            (*Exeunt*

Enter PROVOST, CLAUDIO, JULIET, *and Officers*

Claudio   Fellow, why dost thou show me thus to th'world?
           Bear me to prison, where I am committed.

Provost   I do it not in evil disposition,
           But from Lord Angelo by special charge.

Claudio   Thus can the demi-god Authority   115
           Make us pay down for our offence by weight.

---

94. *stand for seed:* remain for purposes of procreation.
95. *put in:* interceded for.
103. *tapster:* one who draws beer—here a euphemism for 'pimp'.
104–6. *you that . . . the service:* one of the effects of syphilis is blindness, but the
    lines may also refer to the sign of 'Blind Cupid' which was the traditional
    advertisement for a brothel.
107. *Thomas:* a name commonly given to tapsters.
114. *charge:* order.
115. *demi-god Authority:* see *Introduction*, pp. 20–1.
116. *Make . . . weight:* cf. the title 'Measure for Measure'.

The words of heaven: on whom it will, it will;
On whom it will not, so; yet still 'tis just.

Re-enter LUCIO *and the two* Gentlemen

Lucio	Why, how now, Claudio? Whence comes this restraint?
Claudio	From too much liberty, my Lucio, liberty: 120

As surfeit is the father of much fast,
So every scope by the immoderate use
Turns to restraint. Our natures do pursue,
Like rats that ravin down their proper bane,
A thirsty evil; and when we drink, we die.   125

Lucio   If I could speak so wisely under an arrest, I would
send for certain of my creditors: and yet, to say the
truth, I had as lief have the foppery of freedom
as the morality of imprisonment. What's thy
offence, Claudio?   130

Claudio	What but to speak of would offend again.
Lucio	What, is't murder?
Claudio	No.
Lucio	Lechery?
Claudio	Call it so. 135
Provost	Away, sir, you must go.
Claudio	One word, good friend. Lucio, a word with you.
Lucio	A hundred, if they'll do you any good.
	Is lechery so look'd after?
Claudio	Thus stands it with me: upon a true contract 140

117–18. *The words . . . just:* cf. Romans, ix, 15: 'I will have mercy on whom I will
    have mercy, and I will have compassion on whom I will have compassion'.
119. *restraint:* imprisonment, restriction.
121–3. *As surfeit . . . restraint:* Just as over-indulgence leads to fasting, so any free-
    dom used without moderation leads to restriction. *Scope* is ambiguous in
    that it might refer either to Claudio's 'liberty' or to Angelo's 'power'.
123–5. *Our natures . . . evil:* See *Introduction*, p. 10.
124. *ravin:* voraciously devour. *proper:* own. *bane:* death (cf. 'ratsbane', a
    poison).
126–7. *I would . . . creditors:* I would allow myself to be arrested (the impli-
    cation being that Lucio is in debt).
128. *I had as lief:* I would as willingly. *foppery:* irresponsibility.
139. *look'd after:* punished.

54

I got possession of Julietta's bed.
You know the lady; she is fast my wife,
Save that we do the denunciation lack.
Of outward order. This we came not to,
Only for propagation of a dower   145
Remaining in the coffer of her friends,
From whom we thought it meet to hide our love
Till time had made them for us. But it chances
The stealth of our most mutual entertainment
With character too gross is writ on Juliet.   150

Lucio   With child, perhaps?

Claudio   Unhappily, even so.
And the new Deputy now for the Duke—
Whether it be the fault and glimpse of newness,
Or whether that the body public be
A horse whereon the governor doth ride,   155
Who, newly in the seat, that it may know
He can command, lets it straight feel the spur;
Whether the tyranny be in his place,
Or in his eminence that fills it up,
I stagger in—but this new governor   160
Awakes me all the enrolled penalties

140–4. *upon . . . outward order:* See *Commentary 10,* 'Elizabethan Marriage Contracts'.

140. *upon . . .* in consequence of.

142. *fast:* firmly.

143. *denunciation:* formal declaration.

144–8. *This . . . for us:* We did not 'outwardly order' our marriage because we thought that if we kept our love secret her relatives might in time be in favour of our marrying and we would obtain a dowry from them.

149. *mutual entertainment:* intimate pleasure; *mutual* could mean both 'shared' and 'secret'.

150. *character too gross:* too obvious signs (of pregnancy).

153. *fault and glimpse of newness:* error resulting from the dazzling effect of a new office.

154. *body public:* state.

158–9. *Whether . . . it up:* whether the tyranny has resulted from the office or from the man who fills it.

160. *I stagger in:* I hesitate to say.

161. *Awakes me:* resurrects. *enrolled:* recorded (written on a roll of parchment).

Which have, like unscour'd armour, hung by
    th'wall
So long, that nineteen zodiacs have gone round,
And none of them been worn; and, for a name,
Now puts the drowsy and neglected act   165
Freshly on me: 'tis surely for a name.

Lucio   I warrant it is: and thy head stands so tickle on thy
shoulders, that a milkmaid, if she be in love, may
sigh it off. Send after the Duke, and appeal to
him.   170

Claudio   I have done so, but he's not to be found.
I prithee, Lucio, do me this kind service:
This day my sister should the cloister enter
And there receive her approbation.
Acquaint her with the danger of my state;   175
Implore her, in my voice, that she make friends
To the strict deputy; bid herself assay him:
I have great hope in that. For in her youth
There is a prone and speechless dialect,
Such as move men; beside, she hath prosperous art 180
When she will play with reason and discourse,
And well she can persuade.

Lucio   I pray she may: as well for the encouragement
of the like, which else would stand under grievous

---

162. *unscour'd:* uncleaned.
163. *nineteen zodiacs:* nineteen years. The Duke at I, iii, 21 speaks of a period of
    fourteen years. See *Commentary 2*, 'The Text of *Measure for Measure*'.
164. *worn:* in force.
164. *a name:* 'name' could refer to Angelo, meaning 'reputation', or to Claudio,
    meaning 'example'.
167. *stands so tickle:* is so precariously placed.
168–9. *a milkmaid . . . sigh it off:* i.e. the sighs of a lovesick milkmaid would be
    enough to blow off Claudio's head.
173. *cloister:* convent.
174. *receive her approbation:* enter upon her novitiate.
177. *assay:* try, test.
179. *prone:* submissive.   *speechless dialect:* way of communicating without words.
180–2. *she hath . . . persuade:* she has a mastery of rhetoric when she wishes to use it
    and is good at persuading.
183–5. *as well . . . thy life:* as much to encourage similar lechery, which would
    otherwise be heavily threatened, as to save your own life.

	imposition, as for the enjoying of thy life, who I 185
	would be sorry should be thus foolishly lost at
	a game of tick-tack. I'll to her.
Claudio	I thank you, good friend Lucio.
Lucio	Within two hours.
Claudio	Come, officer, away!
	(*Exeunt*

SCENE III. *A Monastery*

Enter DUKE *and* FRIAR THOMAS

Duke	No, holy father, throw away that thought!
	Believe not that the dribbling dart of love
	Can pierce a complete bosom. Why I desire thee
	To give me secret harbour hath a purpose
	More grave and wrinkled than the aims and ends 5
	Of burning youth.
Friar Thomas	May your Grace speak of it?
Duke	My holy sir, none better knows than you
	How I have ever loved the life removed,
	And held in idle price to haunt assemblies
	Where youth, and cost, a witless bravery keeps. 10
	I have deliver'd to Lord Angelo—
	A man of stricture and firm abstinence—
	My absolute power and place here in Vienna,

187. *tick-tack:* a game in which pegs were placed in holes; a humorous reference to sexual intercourse.

1–6. *No . . . Of burning youth:* see *Commentary 11*.
2. *dribbling dart of love:* Cupid's feeble arrow.
3. *complete:* perfectly constituted.
4. *harbour:* lodging, shelter.
9. *idle price:* low esteem.
10. *cost:* luxury. *witless bravery:* foolish ostentation. *keeps:* maintain.
12. *stricture:* strictness. *firm:* rigid.

And he supposes me travell'd to Poland;
For so I have strew'd it in the common ear,   15
And so it is received. Now, pious sir,
You will demand of me, why I do this.

Friar Thomas   Gladly, my lord.

Duke   We have strict statutes and most biting laws,
The needful bits and curbs to headstrong weeds,   20
Which for this fourteen years we have let slip,
Even like an o'er-grown lion in a cave
That goes not out to prey. Now, as fond fathers,
Having bound up the threatening twigs of birch,
Only to stick it in their children's sight   25
For terror, not to use, in time the rod
Becomes more mock'd than fear'd: so our decrees,
Dead to infliction, to themselves are dead,
And Liberty plucks Justice by the nose,
The baby beats the nurse, and quite athwart   30
Goes all decorum.

Friar Thomas   It rested in your Grace
To unloose this tied-up justice when you pleased;
And it in you more dreadful would have seem'd
Than in Lord Angelo.

Duke   I do fear, too dreadful.
Sith 'twas my fault to give the people scope,   35
'Twould be my tyranny to strike and gall them

---

15. *strew'd:* spread.
20. *The needful . . . weeds:* 'weeds' is often emended to 'steeds'. However, this
    speech of the Duke's contains a number of contrived and unrelated meta-
    phors, and it is consistent with the style that one of the metaphors should itself
    be mixed.
21. *fourteen:* cf. I, ii, 164. *let slip:* disregarded.
23. *fond:* foolish.
24. *bound up:* prepared.
27–8. *so . . . are dead:* so our laws, not being enforced, are ignored.
30–1. *quite athwart . . . decorum:* social order has gone completely awry.
35. *Sith:* since. *scope:* freedom, licence.
36–9. *'Twould . . . punishment:* it would be tyrannical of me to punish them for
    what I encouraged them to do: for when we allow evil deeds to remain
    unpunished it is encouraging people to commit them.

For what I bid them do: for we bid this be done,
When evil deeds have their permissive pass,
And not the punishment. Therefore indeed, my
    father,
I have on Angelo imposed the office;   40
Who may in th'ambush of my name strike home,
And yet my nature never in the fight
To do in slander. And to behold his sway,
I will, as 'twere a brother of your order,
Visit both prince and people. Therefore, I prithee, 45
Supply me with the habit, and instruct me
How I may formally in person bear
Like a true friar. Moe reasons for this action
At our more leisure shall I render you;
Only this one: Lord Angelo is precise;   50
Stands at a guard with Envy; scarce confesses
That his blood flows, or that his appetite
Is more to bread than stone. Hence shall we see,
If power change purpose, what our seemers be.
                                    (*Exeunt*

SCENE IV. *A Nunnery*

Enter ISABELLA *and* FRANCISCA, *a nun*

Isabella   And have you nuns no farther privileges?
Francisca   Are not these large enough?

41–3. *Who . . . slander:* Angelo, using the Duke's authority, will be able to punish sin without bringing the Ducal office into disrepute.
43. *sway:* rule.
45. *prince:* i.e. Angelo.
47. *formally in person bear:* conduct myself.
48. *Moe:* more.
50. *precise:* strict in morals, puritanical. (See *Commentary 12*, 'Puritans'.)
51. *Stands at a guard with Envy:* keeps a strong defence against malicious report, i.e. is very careful of his reputation.
51–2. *scarce . . . flows:* hardly admits that he has a sensual side to his nature.
52–3. *or that . . . stone:* or that he could succumb to temptation. (See *Commentary 13*, 'Angelo and Temptation'.)

Isabella	Yes, truly: I speak not as desiring more,
	But rather wishing a more strict restraint
	Upon the sisterhood, the votarists of Saint Clare. 5
Lucio	(*Within*) Ho! Peace be in this place!
Isabella	Who's that which calls?
Francisca	It is a man's voice. Gentle Isabella,
	Turn you the key, and know his business of him:
	You may, I may not; you are yet unsworn:
	When you have vow'd, you must not speak with
	men 10
	But in the presence of the prioress:
	Then, if you speak, you must not show your face;
	Or if you show your face, you must not speak.
	He calls again: I pray you, answer him.
Isabella	Peace and prosperity! Who is't that calls? 15

Enter LUCIO

Lucio	Hail virgin, if you be, as those cheek-roses
	Proclaim you are no less! Can you so stead me
	As bring me to the sight of Isabella,
	A novice of this place, and the fair sister
	To her unhappy brother Claudio? 20
Isabella	Why 'her unhappy brother'? Let me ask,
	The rather for I now must make you know
	I am that Isabella, and his sister.
Lucio	Gentle and fair. Your brother kindly greets you.
	Not to be weary with you, he's in prison. 25
Isabella	Woe me! For what?
Lucio	For that which, if myself might be his judge,
	He should receive his punishment in thanks:

---

5. *votarists:* nuns. *Saint Clare:* a friend of Saint Francis and the founder of the
   order of the Poor Clares.
16. *cheek-roses:* blushes.
17. *stead:* help.
22. *The rather for:* more especially since.
24. *kindly:* with affection, but also implying 'in kinship'.
25. *weary:* long-winded.

	He hath got his friend with child.	
Isabella	Sir, make me not your story.	
Lucio	'Tis true.	30

I would not, though 'tis my familiar sin
With maids to seem the lapwing, and to jest,
Tongue far from heart, play with all virgins so.
I hold you as a thing enskied and sainted;
By your renouncement, an immortal spirit,   35
And to be talk'd with in sincerity,
As with a saint.

| Isabella | You do blaspheme the good, in mocking me. | |
| Lucio | Do not believe it. Fewness and truth, 'tis thus: | |

Your brother and his lover have embraced;   40
As those that feed grow full, as blossoming time
That from the seedness the bare fallow brings
To teeming foison, even so her plenteous womb
Expresseth his full tilth and husbandry.

Isabella	Some one with child by him? My cousin Juliet?	45
Lucio	Is she your cousin?	
Isabella	Adoptedly, as schoolmaids change their names	

By vain though apt affection.

Lucio	She it is.	
Isabella	O, let him marry her!	
Lucio	This is the point.	

The duke is very strangely gone from hence;   50

29. *friend:* girlfriend.
30. *make me not your story:* do not mock me.
31. *familiar:* habitual.
32. *to seem the lapwing:* to be insincere. Lapwings were proverbial for insincerity, a reputation gained through their wiliness in keeping beasts of prey from their nests.
34. *enskied:* placed in Heaven. Lucio's sarcasm is not lost on Isabella.
35. *renouncement:* giving up the world.
38. *the good:* i.e. those who are truly saintly, in contrast to herself.
39. *Fewness and truth:* the truth in a few words.
42. *seedness:* sowing with seed.   *bare fallow:* harrowed ground.
43. *teeming foison:* plentiful harvest.
44. *tilth and husbandry:* cultivation (with a pun on 'husband').
48. *vain though apt:* foolish yet fitting.

Bore many gentlemen, myself being one,
In hand, and hope of action: but we do learn,
By those that know the very nerves of state,
His givings-out were of an infinite distance
From his true-meant design. Upon his place,　　55
And with full line of his authority,
Governs Lord Angelo; a man whose blood
Is very snow-broth; one who never feels
The wanton stings and motions of the sense,
But doth rebate and blunt his natural edge　　60
With profits of the mind, study and fast.
He, to give fear to use and liberty,
Which have for long run by the hideous law
As mice by lions, hath pick'd out an act,
Under whose heavy sense your brother's life　　65
Falls into forfeit: he arrests him on it,
And follows close the rigour of the statute
To make him an example. All hope is gone,
Unless you have the grace by your fair prayer
To soften Angelo. And that's my pith of busi-
　　　　ness　　　　　　　　　　　　　　　70
'Twixt you and your poor brother.

Isabella　　Doth he so seek his life?

51-2. *Bore . . . action:* deluded many gentlemen, including myself, into hoping
that there would be military service.
53. *the very nerves of state:* i.e. inner state secrets.
54-5. *His givings-out . . . design:* the reasons which he gave were very different
from his real intentions.
56. *full line:* complete freedom.
58. *snow-broth:* melted snow.
59. *wanton stings:* lascivious urges.　*motions of the sense:* inward promptings of
sexual desire.
60. *rebate:* lessen.　*edge:* keenness (of desire).
61. *profits of the mind:* things which will improve the mind.
62. *to give fear to:* to frighten.　*use and liberty:* habitual licentiousness.
63. *hideous:* terrifying.
64. *pick'd out an act:* revived a law.
65. *heavy sense:* cruel terms.
66. *Falls into forfeit:* is lost to the law.
70. *my pith of business:* the essence of my business.

Lucio	Has censur'd him
	Already; and (as I hear) the Provost hath
	A warrant for's execution.
Isabella	Alas! What poor ability's in me 75
	To do him good?
Lucio	Assay the power you have.
Isabella	My power? Alas, I doubt—
Lucio	Our doubts are traitors,
	And make us lose the good we oft might win
	By fearing to attempt. Go to Lord Angelo,
	And let him learn to know, when maidens sue, 80
	Men give like gods; but when they weep and
	kneel,
	All their petitions are as freely theirs
	As they themselves would owe them.
Isabella	I'll see what I can do.
Lucio	But speedily.
Isabella	I will about it straight, 85
	No longer staying but to give the Mother
	Notice of my affair. I humbly thank you.
	Commend me to my brother: soon at night
	I'll send him certain word of my success.
Lucio	I take my leave of you.
Isabella	Good sir, adieu. 90

(Exeunt

72. *censur'd*: sentenced.
73. *Provost*: officer charged with punishing offenders.
76. *Assay*: try.
80. *sue*: plead.
82. *their petitions*: the things they ask for.
83. *As they themselves would owe them:* as if they (the maidens) owned them themselves.
86. *the Mother:* the head of the nunnery.
88. *soon at night:* early this evening.
89. *my success:* the result of my endeavour.

ACT II

SCENE I. *A Court of Law*

Enter ANGELO *and* ESCALUS, *followed by the* PROVOST, *a* JUSTICE, *and other attendants*

Angelo	We must not make a scarecrow of the law,
	Setting it up to fear the birds of prey,
	And let it keep one shape till custom make it
	Their perch and not their terror.
Escalus	Ay, but yet
	Let us be keen, and rather cut a little, 5
	Than fall, and bruise to death. Alas, this gentle-
	man,
	Whom I would save, had a most noble father.
	Let but your honour know—
	Whom I believe to be most strait in virtue—
	That, in the working of your own affections, 10
	Had time cohered with place, or place with
	wishing,
	Or that the resolute acting of your blood
	Could have attain'd th'effect of your own pur-
	pose,
	Whether you had not sometime in your life
	Err'd in this point, which now you censure him, 15
	And pull'd the law upon you.
Angelo	'Tis one thing to be tempted, Escalus,

2. *fear:* frighten.

5–6. *Let us . . . death:* let us use the law as a surgeon's knife (which will promote cure) and not as a bludgeon which only deals out death.   *keen:* sharp.

6. *fall:* let fall, 'fell'.

8–16. *Let . . . you:* Escalus asks Angelo to consider whether or not at sometime in his life, given temptation and opportunity, his own physical desires might have driven him to offend against the law in the same way as Claudio, whom he is now censuring.

9. *strait:* strict.

10. *affections:* physical desires.

11. *cohered:* agreed.

12–13. *the resolute acting . . . your own purpose:* the strong urges of your desires could have achieved their aim.

Another thing to fall. I not deny
The jury passing on the prisoner's life
May in the sworn twelve have a thief or two   20
Guiltier than him they try. What's open made to
    justice,
That justice seizes. What knows the laws
That thieves do pass on thieves? 'Tis very
    pregnant,
The jewel that we find, we stoop and take't,
Because we see it; but what we do not see,   25
We tread upon, and never think of it.
You may not so extenuate his offence
For I have had such faults; but rather tell me,
When I, that censure him, do so offend,
Let mine own judgement pattern out my death,   30
And nothing come in partial. Sir, he must die.

Escalus	Be it as your wisdom will.
Angelo	Where is the provost?
Provost	Here, if it like your honour.
Angelo	See that Claudio

Be executed by nine tomorrow morning:
Bring him his confessor, let him be prepared,   35
For that's the utmost of his pilgrimage.

                            (*Exit Provost*

Escalus   (*Aside*) Well, heaven forgive him, and forgive us
            all.

18. *I not:* I do not.
19. *passing:* passing sentence.
21. *open made:* laid open.
22–3. *What . . . thieves:* how can the law know that thieves sit among the jury?
23. *pregnant:* clear.
24–6. *The jewel . . . of it:* see *Introduction*, pp. 12–13.
27. *so:* in this way.   *extenuate:* mitigate.
28. *For:* because.
29. *censure:* sentence.
30–1. *Let . . . in partial:* let me be sentenced according to my own decree on
    Claudio, without any special pleading being introduced on my behalf.
35. *let him be prepared:* let his soul be made ready.
36. *utmost of his pilgrimage:* final stage of his life's journey.

Some rise by sin, and some by virtue fall:
Some run from brakes of ice, and answer none,
And some condemned for a fault alone.   40

Enter ELBOW *and* Officers, *with* FROTH *and* POMPEY *under arrest*

Elbow	Come, bring them away. If these be good people in a commonweal that do nothing but use their abuses in common houses, I know no law: bring them away.
Angelo	How now sir! What's your name? And what's the matter? 45
Elbow	If it please your honour, I am the poor Duke's constable, and my name is Elbow: I do lean upon justice, sir, and do bring in here before your good honour two notorious benefactors. 50
Angelo	Benefactors? Well, what benefactors are they? Are they not malefactors?
Elbow	If it please your honour, I know not well what they are: but precise villains they are, that I am sure of, and void of all profanation in the world 55 that good Christians ought to have.
Escalus	This comes off well: here's a wise officer.
Angelo	Go to: what quality are they of? Elbow is your name? Why dost thou not speak, Elbow?
Pompey	He cannot, sir: he's out at elbow. 60
Angelo	What are you, sir?

39–40. *Some run . . . a fault alone:* some make no attempt to live virtuously and go unpunished, while others are punished for a single offence. (See *Commentary 14.*)
41. *away:* along.
42. *commonweal:* commonwealth. *use:* practise.
43. *common houses:* brothels.
50. *benefactors:* Elbow means 'malefactors'.
54. *precise:* 'neither more nor less than' (but the word could also mean 'puritanical'; cf. I, iii, 50).
55. *void:* devoid. *profanation:* impious conduct. Elbow means the opposite.
57. *This comes off well:* this is good entertainment.
58. *Go to:* a term of rebuke. To Angelo this is no laughing matter. *quality:* profession.
60. *he's out at elbow:* he is speechless (like an actor with a worn-out costume).

Elbow	He, sir? A tapster, sir; parcel-bawd; one that serves a bad woman; whose house, sir, was, as they say, plucked down in the suburbs; and now she professes a hot-house, which, I think, is a very ill 65 house too.
Escalus	How know you that?
Elbow	My wife, sir, whom I detest before heaven and your honour—
Escalus	How? Thy wife? 70
Elbow	Ay, sir: whom, I thank heaven, is an honest woman—
Escalus	Dost thou detest her therefore?
Elbow	I say, sir, I will detest myself also, as well as she, that this house, if it be not a bawd's house, it is pity 75 of her life, for it is a naughty house.
Escalus	How dost thou know that, constable?
Elbow	Marry, sir, by my wife, who, if she had been a woman cardinally given, might have been accused in fornication, adultery, and all uncleanli- 80 ness there.
Escalus	By the woman's means?
Elbow	Ay, sir, by Mistress Overdone's means; but as she spit in his face, so she defied him.
Pompey	Sir, if it please your honour, this is not so. 85
Elbow	Prove it before these varlets here, thou honourable man, prove it.
Escalus	Do you hear how he misplaces?
Pompey	Sir, she came in great with child; and longing,

62. *parcel-bawd:* partly bawd.
64. *plucked down:* demolished.
64–5. *she professes a hothouse:* she maintains that she runs a bathhouse.
65. *ill:* infamous.
68. *detest:* Elbow means 'protest'.
75–6. *it is pity of her life:* it is a sad thing.
76. *naughty:* wicked.
79. *cardinally:* Elbow means 'carnally'.
83. *by Mistress Overdone's means:* i.e. by her pimp, Pompey.
88. *misplaces:* uses words in the wrong place.

	saving your honour's reverence, for stewed 90 prunes; sir we had but two in the house, which at that very distant time stood, as it were, in a fruit-dish, a dish of some three-pence; your honours have seen such dishes; they are not china dishes, but very good dishes— 95
Escalus	Go to, go to: no matter for the dish, sir.
Pompey	No, indeed, sir, not of a pin; you are therein in the right: but to the point. As I say, this Mistress Elbow, being, as I say, with child, and being great-bellied, and longing, as I said, for prunes; 100 and having but two in the dish, as I said, Master Froth here, this very man, having eaten the rest, as I said, and, as I say, paying for them very honestly; for, as you know, Master Froth, I could not give you three-pence again. 105
Froth	No, indeed.
Pompey	Very well: you being then, if you be remembered, cracking the stones of the foresaid prunes—
Froth	Ay, so I did indeed.
Pompey	Why, very well: I telling you then, if you be 110 remembered, that such a one and such a one were past cure of the thing you wot of, unless they kept very good diet, as I told you—
Froth	All this is true.
Pompey	Why, very well, then— 115
Escalus	Come, you are a tedious fool! To the purpose: what was done to Elbow's wife, that he hath cause to complain of? Come me to what was done to her.

90. *stewed prunes:* a dish traditionally served in Elizabethan brothels.
92. *distant time:* he probably means 'instant in time'.
97. *not of a pin:* not at all.
105. *again:* back (as change).
107–8 *be remembered:* remember.
111–12. *were past cure of the thing you wot of:* another allusion to venereal disease.
112. *wot:* know.
117. *done:* Pompey again takes up the bawdy meaning: cf. I, ii, 82.
118. *Come me:* bring me.

Pompey	Sir, your honour cannot come to that yet.	120
Escalus	No sir, nor I mean it not.	
Pompey	Sir, but you shall come to it, by your honour's leave. And, I beseech you, look into Master Froth here, sir; a man of fourscore pound a year, whose father died at Hallowmas—was't not at Hallow- mas, Master Froth?	125
Froth	All-hallond eve.	
Pompey	Why, very well; I hope here be truths. He, sir, sitting, as I say, in a lower chair, sir, 'twas in the Bunch of Grapes, where, indeed, you have a delight to sit, have you not?	130
Froth	I have so, because it is an open room, and good for winter.	
Pompey	Why, very well, then; I hope here be truths.	
Angelo	This will last out a night in Russia When nights are longest there: I'll take my leave, And leave you to the hearing of the cause; Hoping you'll find good cause to whip them all.	135
Escalus	I think no less. Good morrow to your lordship.	

(*Exit Angelo*

	Now, sir, come on. What was done to Elbow's wife, once more?	140
Pompey	Once, sir? There was nothing done to her once.	
Elbow	I beseech you, sir, ask him what this man did to my wife.	
Pompey	I beseech your honour, ask me.	145
Escalus	Well, sir, what did this gentleman to her?	
Pompey	I beseech you, sir, look in this gentleman's face.	

121. *nor I mean it not:* I do not mean 'done' in the way that you have interpreted it.
124. *fourscore pound a year:* an income to make Froth socially respectable; cf. Escalus's plea for Claudio, II, i, 7.
125. *Hallowmas:* All Saints' Day, 1 November.
127. *All-hallond eve:* Vigil of All Saints' Day, 31 October.
129. *lower chair:* possibly a seat reserved for people of some importance.
130. *the Bunch of Grapes:* Names were often given to the different rooms in an Elizabethan tavern.
132. *an open room:* a public room in which there would probably be a fire.
140. *done:* cf. line 117.

	Good Master Froth, look upon his honour; 'tis for	
	a good purpose. Doth your honour mark his face?	
Escalus	Ay, sir, very well.	150
Pompey	Nay, I beseech you, mark it well.	
Escalus	Well, I do so.	
Pompey	Doth your honour see any harm in his face?	
Escalus	Why, no.	

Pompey   I'll be supposed upon a book, his face is the 155
worst thing about him. Good, then; if his face be
the worst thing about him, how could Master
Froth do the constable's wife any harm? I would
know that of your honour.

Escalus   He's in the right. Constable, what say you to it? 160

Elbow   First, and it like you, the house is a respected
house; next, this is a respected fellow; and his
mistress is a respected woman.

Pompey   By this hand, sir, his wife is a more respected
person than any of us all.   165

Elbow   Varlet, thou liest; thou liest, wicked varlet! The
time is yet to come that she was ever respected
with man, woman, or child.

Pompey   Sir, she was respected with him before he married
with her.   170

Escalus   Which is the wiser here, Justice or Iniquity? Is
this true?

Elbow   O thou caitiff! O thou varlet! O thou wicked
Hannibal! I respected with her before I was
married to her! If ever I was respected with her, 175

---

155. *supposed:* he means 'deposed', i.e. 'sworn'.
161. *and:* if. *respected:* Elbow may mean either 'suspected' or 'disreputable', the
opposite of 'respected'.
171. *Justice or Iniquity:* both were personifications in Morality plays. See *Introduction*, pp. 32–4.
173. *caitiff:* wretch.
174. *Hannibal:* Elbow may mean 'cannibal'. However, like the more famous
Pompey, Hannibal was a general.

	or she with me, let not your worship think me the poor Duke's officer. Prove this, thou wicked Hannibal, or I'll have mine action of battery on thee.	
Escalus	If he took you a box o' th' ear, you might have your action of slander too.	180
Elbow	Marry, I thank your good worship for it. What is't your worship's pleasure I shall do with this wicked caitiff?	
Escalus	Truly, officer, because he hath some offences in him that thou wouldst discover if thou couldst, let him continue in his courses till thou know'st what they are.	185
Elbow	Marry, I thank your worship for it. Thou seest, thou wicked varlet, now, what's come upon thee. Thou art to continue now, thou varlet, thou art to continue.	190
Escalus	Where were you born, friend?	
Froth	Here in Vienna, sir.	
Escalus	Are you of fourscore pounds a year?	195
Froth	Yes, and't please you, sir.	
Escalus	So. What trade are you of, sir?	
Pompey	A tapster, a poor widow's tapster.	
Escalus	Your mistress' name?	
Pompey	Mistress Overdone.	200
Escalus	Hath she had any more than one husband?	
Pompey	Nine, sir; Overdone by the last.	
Escalus	Nine! Come hither to me, Master Froth. Master Froth, I would not have you acquainted with tapsters: they will draw you, Master Froth, and you will hang them. Get you gone, and let me hear no	205

---

180. *took you:* struck you.

202. *Overdone by the last:* the culmination of Pompey's punning on the word 'done'.

205. *draw:* a quibble on 'drawing' beer and disembowelling. Traitors were 'hanged, drawn and quartered'.

	more of you.	
Froth	I thank your worship. For mine own part, I never come into any room in a taphouse, but I am drawn in.	210
Escalus	Well, no more of it, Master Froth: farewell. (*Exit Froth*) Come you hither to me, Master tapster. What's your name, Master tapster?	
Pompey	Pompey.	
Escalus	What else?	215
Pompey	Bum, sir.	
Escalus	Troth, and your bum is the greatest thing about you; so that, in the beastliest sense, you are Pompey the Great. Pompey, you are partly a bawd, Pompey, howsoever you colour it in being a tapster, are you not? Come, tell me true, it shall be the better for you.	220
Pompey	Truly, sir, I am a poor fellow that would live.	
Escalus	How would you live, Pompey? By being a bawd? What do you think of the trade, Pompey? Is it a lawful trade?	225
Pompey	If the law would allow it, sir.	
Escalus	But the law will not allow it, Pompey; nor it shall not be allowed in Vienna.	
Pompey	Does your worship mean to geld and splay all the youth of the city?	230
Escalus	No, Pompey.	
Pompey	Truly, sir, in my poor opinion, they will to't, then. If your worship will take order for the drabs and the knaves, you need not to fear the bawds.	235
Escalus	There are pretty orders beginning, I can tell you:	

218. *beastliest:* most disgusting.
219. *bawd:* procurer or procuress; since 1700 used only of women.
220. *colour it:* disguise it.
230. *geld and splay:* terms used for the castration of male and female animals respectively.
234. *take order:* make arrangements.   *drabs:* prostitutes.
235. *knaves:* rascals.
236. *pretty orders:* fine arrangements.

it is but heading and hanging.

Pompey   If you head and hang all that offend that way but
for ten year together, you'll be glad to give out a
commission for more heads: if this law hold in 240
Vienna ten year, I'll rent the fairest house in it
after threepence a bay. If you live to see this come
to pass, say Pompey told you so.

Escalus   Thank you, good Pompey; and, in requital of
your prophecy, hark you: I advise you, let me not 245
find you before me again upon any complaint
whatsoever; no, not for dwelling where you do. If
I do, Pompey, I shall beat you to your tent, and
prove a shrewd Caesar to you: in plain dealing,
Pompey, I shall have you whipped. So, for this 250
time, Pompey, fare you well.

Pompey   I thank your worship for your good counsel;
(*Aside*) but I shall follow it as the flesh and fortune
shall better determine.
Whip me? No, no, let carman whip his jade;   255
The valiant heart 's not whipt out of his trade.

(*Exit*

Escalus   Come hither to me, Master Elbow: come hither,
Master constable. How long have you been in
this place of constable?

Elbow   Seven year and a half, sir.   260

Escalus   I thought, by your readiness in the office, you had
continued in it some time. You say seven years
together?

237. *heading:* beheading.
242. *after threepence a bay:* at the rate of threepence a division. (Some Elizabethan
    houses were divided into separate *bays.*)
244. *requital:* repayment.
249. *shrewd:* severe. *Caesar:* the vanquisher of Pompey the Great.
253-4. *but I shall . . . determine:* whether or not I follow your advice will
    depend upon the state of the prostitution market.
255. *carman:* carter. *jade:* ill-conditioned horse.
261. *readiness:* efficiency.
263. *together:* in succession.

Elbow	And a half, sir.
Escalus	Alas, it hath been great pains to you. They do 265 you wrong to put you so oft upon 't! Are there not men in your ward sufficient to serve it?
Elbow	Faith, sir, few of any wit in such matters. As they are chosen, they are glad to choose me for them; I do it for some piece of money, and go through 270 with all.
Escalus	Look you bring me in the names of some six or seven, the most sufficient of your parish.
Elbow	To your worship's house, sir?
Escalus	To my house. Fare you well. (*Exit Elbow*) What's 275 o'clock, think you?
Justice	Eleven, sir.
Escalus	I pray you home to dinner with me.
Justice	I humbly thank you.
Escalus	It grieves me for the death of Claudio; 280 But there's no remedy.
Justice	Lord Angelo is severe.
Escalus	It is but needful. Mercy is not itself, that oft looks so; Pardon is still the nurse of second woe. But yet—poor Claudio! There is no remedy. 285 Come, sir. (*Exeunt*

266. *to put you so oft upon 't:* to elect you to the office of constable so often.
267. *ward:* division of the city. *sufficient:* able.
268. *wit:* intelligence.
270. *some piece of money:* a little money.
278. *dinner:* the Elizabethans had their main meal of the day shortly before noon.
283–4. *Mercy . . . woe:* that which seems like mercy is often not merciful in that it may encourage further offence.

Scene II. *Angelo's House*

Enter Provost *and a* Servant

Servant	He's hearing of a cause: he will come straight;
	I'll tell him of you.
Provost	Pray you, do. (*Exit Servant*) I'll know
	His pleasure, may be he will relent. Alas,
	He hath but as offended in a dream.
	All sects, all ages smack of this vice, and he 5
	To die for't!

Enter Angelo

Angelo	Now, what's the matter, provost?
Provost	Is it your will Claudio shall die tomorrow?
Angelo	Did not I tell thee yea? Hadst thou not order?
	Why dost thou ask again?
Provost	Lest I might be too rash.
	Under your good correction, I have seen 10
	When, after execution, Judgement hath
	Repented o'er his doom.
Angelo	Go to; let that be mine;
	Do you your office, or give up your place,
	And you shall well be spared.
Provost	I crave your honour's pardon.
	What shall be done, sir, with the groaning
	Juliet? 15
	She's very near her hour.

1. *straight:* immediately.
3, 4. *he:* the 'he' refers first to Angelo and then to Claudio.
4. *but as offended in a dream:* the Provost compares Claudio's offence to an offence committed in a nightmare.
5. *sects:* classes. *ages:* both young and old, past and present. *smack:* partake, taste.
10. *Under your good correction:* at the risk of offending you.
12. *doom:* sentence. *mine:* my concern.
13. *office:* duty.
14. *And you shall be well spared:* and we could easily do without you. *crave:* beg.
15. *groaning:* i.e. in labour.
16. *She's very near her hour:* she is about to have her child.

Angelo	Dispose of her To some more fitter place, and that with speed.

Re-enter Servant

Servant	Here is the sister of the man condemn'd Desires access to you.	
Angelo	Hath he a sister?	
Provost	Ay, my good lord, a very virtuous maid, And to be shortly of a sisterhood, If not already.	20
Angelo	Well, let her be admitted.	

(*Exit Servant*

See you the fornicatress be removed;
Let her have needful, but not lavish, means;
There shall be order for 't.

Enter ISABELLA *and* LUCIO

Provost	Save your honour!	25
Angelo	Stay a little while. (*To Isab*) You're welcome: what's your will?	
Isabella	I am a woeful suitor to your honour, Please but your honour hear me.	
Angelo	Well: what's your suit?	
Isabella	There is a vice that most I do abhor, And most desire should meet the blow of justice; For which I would not plead, but that I must; For which I must not plead, but that I am At war 'twixt will and will not.	30
Angelo	Well: the matter?	
Isabella	I have a brother is condemn'd to die: I do beseech you, let it be his fault And not my brother.	35

19. *access:* admittance.
24. *needful:* necessary. *means:* assistance.
25. *Save:* God save.
31–3. *For which . . . will not:* Isabella is torn between her abhorrence of lust and
her affection for her brother.

Provost	(*Aside*) Heaven give thee moving graces!
Angelo	Condemn the fault and not the actor of it?
	Why, every fault's condemn'd ere it be done:
	Mine were the very cipher of a function,
	To fine the faults whose fine stands in record, 40
	And let go by the actor.
Isabella	O just but severe law!
	I had a brother, then. Heaven keep your honour.
Lucio	(*Aside to Isab*) Give't not o'er so: to him again,
	entreat him;
	Kneel down before him, hand upon his gown.
	You are too cold. If you should need a pin, 45
	You could not with more tame a tongue desire it.
	To him, I say.
Isabella	Must he needs die?
Angelo	Maiden, no remedy.
Isabella	Yet I do think that you might pardon him,
	And neither heaven nor man grieve at the mercy. 50
Angelo	I will not do 't.
Isabella	But can you, if you would?
Angelo	Look, what I will not, that I cannot do.
Isabella	But might you do't, and do the world no wrong,
	If so your heart were touch'd with that remorse
	As mine is to him?
Angelo	He's sentenced, 'tis too late. 55
Lucio	(*Aside to Isab*) You are too cold.
Isabella	Too late? Why, no. I, that do speak a word,
	May call it back again. Well, believe this:

38. *Why . . . done:* the law condemns all faults before they are committed.
39–41. *Mine . . . actor:* my position would be non-existent if I had merely to attend to offences which are already recorded as offences and not to the people who commit them.
39. *cipher:* zero.
40. *fire:* punish.
42. *I had a brother, then:* Isabella means that her brother is as good as dead already.
43. *Give't not o'er so:* don't give up so easily.
51. *But can you:* do you have the authority?
53–5. *But might you . . . to him:* but could you not pardon him without wronging society if your heart, like mine, was touched by compassion?

No ceremony that to great ones 'longs,
Not the king's crown, nor the deputed sword,   60
The marshal's truncheon, nor the judge's robe,
Become them with one half so good a grace
As mercy does.
If he had been as you, and you as he,
You would have slipt like him, but he, like you, 65
Would not have been so stern.

Angelo   Pray you be gone.
Isabella   I would to heaven I had your potency,
And you were Isabel! Should it then be thus?
No; I would tell what 'twere to be a judge,
And what a prisoner.

Lucio   (*Aside to Isab*) Ay, touch him; there's the vein. 70
Angelo   Your brother is a forfeit of the law,
And you but waste your words.

Isabella   Alas, alas!
Why, all the souls that were were forfeit once,
And He that might the vantage best have took
Found out the remedy. How would you be,   75
If He, which is the top of judgement, should
But judge you as you are? O, think on that,
And mercy then will breathe within your lips,
Like man new made.

59–63. *No ceremony . . . As mercy does:* no part of the external show which
    accompanies authority is as becoming as mercy.
59. *'longs:* belongs.
60. *deputed sword:* emblem of high state appointment, cf. III, ii, 264.
61. *marshal's truncheon:* symbol of military command.
62. *grace:* used here in both a spiritual and a physical sense.
67. *potency:* power.
70. *there's the vein:* that's the style.
71. *is a forfeit of the law:* is handed over to the law.
73. *forfeit:* lost.
74–5. *And He . . . remedy:* and Christ, who might have gained most by the loss,
    found a way to save them.
76. *He, which is the top of judgement:* God, the supreme judge.
77–9. *O, think . . . Like man new made:* think of yourself as one who will be
    judged by God, and his mercy will pass through your lips as though you were
    reborn.

Angelo   Be you content, fair maid;
It is the law, not I, condemn your brother: 80
Were he my kinsman, brother, or my son,
It should be thus with him: he must die tomorrow.

Isabella   Tomorrow? O, that's sudden! Spare him, spare
him!
He's not prepared for death. Even for our kitchens
We kill the fowl of season: shall we serve
heaven   85
With less respect than we do minister
To our gross selves? Good, good my lord, bethink
you:
Who is it that hath died for this offence?
There's many have committed it.

Lucio   (Aside to Isab) Ay, well said.

Angelo   The law hath not been dead, though it hath slept: 90
Those many had not dared to do that evil
If the first that did th'edict infringe
Had answer'd for his deed. Now 'tis awake,
Takes note of what is done, and, like a prophet,
Looks in a glass that shows what future evils—   95
Either now, or by remissness new-conceived,
And so in progress to be hatch'd and born—
Are now to have no successive degrees,

83. sudden: soon.
85. the fowl of season: the bird appropriate to the time of year.
85-7. shall we . . . our gross selves: shall we supply souls to Heaven with less
consideration than we give to supplying ourselves with food?
87. bethink you: consider.
90-9. The law . . . to end: Angelo tells Isabella that the law, awake once more,
has the dual function of punishing those offences which were committed
while it slept and, by so doing, of putting an end to future offences before
they have an opportunity to develop. (It is characteristic of Angelo that he
should use a metaphor in which 'unborn children' are associated with 'evil
deeds'.)
91. that evil: fornication.
95. a glass: a magic mirror which shows the future. evils: sins.
96. Either now, or by remissness new-conceived: either already in existence or
recently conceived through negligence.
98. no successive degrees: no future stages of development.

	But, ere they live, to end.	
Isabella	Yet show some pity.	
Angelo	I show it most of all when I show justice;	100
	For then I pity those I do not know,	
	Which a dismiss'd offence would after gall;	
	And do him right that, answering one foul wrong,	
	Lives not to act another. Be satisfied;	
	Your brother dies tomorrow; be content.	105
Isabella	So you must be the first that gives this sentence,	
	And he, that suffers. O, it is excellent	
	To have a giant's strength, but it is tyrannous	
	To use it like a giant.	
Lucio	(*Aside to Isab*) That's well said.	
Isabella	Could great men thunder	110
	As Jove himself does, Jove would ne'er be quiet,	
	For every pelting, petty officer	
	Would use his heaven for thunder.	
	Nothing but thunder! Merciful Heaven,	
	Thou rather with thy sharp and sulphurous bolt	115
	Splits the unwedgeable and gnarled oak	
	Than the soft myrtle: but man, proud man,	
	Dressed in a little brief authority,	
	Most ignorant of what he's most assured—	
	His glassy essence—like an angry ape	120
	Plays such fantastic tricks before high heaven	
	As makes the angels weep; who, with our spleens,	
	Would all themselves laugh mortal.	

102. *gall:* hurt.
103–4. *And . . . another:* and I do a good service to the offender by seeing that he does not live to commit other offences.
112. *pelting:* paltry.
115. *bolt:* thunderbolt.
118. *brief:* short-lived.
120. *His glassy essence:* i.e. man's soul (although it has been suggested that the 'glassy essence' is man's frail mortal body, itself a reflection of his divine spirit).
122. *our spleens:* the spleen was regarded as the seat of both melancholy and laughter.
123. *laugh mortal:* Isabella means that the angels would laugh so much that they would become mortal.

Lucio	(*Aside to Isab*) O, to him, to him, wench! He will relent;
	He's coming; I perceive 't.
Provost	(*Aside*) Pray heaven she win him! 125
Isabella	We cannot weigh our brother with ourself.
	Great men may jest with saints: 'tis wit in them,
	But in the less foul profanation.
Lucio	(*To Isabella*) Thou'rt i' th' right, girl; more o' that.
Isabella	That in the captain's but a choleric word, 130
	Which in the soldier is flat blasphemy.
Lucio	(*Aside to Isab*) Art avised o' that? More on't.
Angelo	Why do you put these sayings upon me?
Isabella	Because authority, though it err like others,
	Hath yet a kind of medicine in itself 135
	That skins the vice o' the top. Go to your bosom,
	Knock there, and ask your heart what it doth know
	That's like my brother's fault. If it confess
	A natural guiltiness such as is his,
	Let it not sound a thought upon your tongue 140
	Against my brother's life.
Angelo	(*Aside*) She speaks, and 'tis
	Such sense, that my sense breeds with it. Fare you well.
Isabella	Gentle my lord, turn back.
Angelo	I will bethink me. Come again tomorrow.
Isabella	Hark how I'll bribe you: good my lord, turn back. 145
Angelo	How? Bribe me?

126. *We cannot . . . ourself:* we cannot apply to others the same standards which we apply to ourselves.
127. *jest:* make merry. *wit:* clever humour.
128. *foul profanation:* disgusting impiety.
130. *choleric:* angry.
131. *flat:* downright.
132. *avised:* informed.
133. *Why . . . upon me:* why do you apply these sayings to me?
134-6. *authority . . . o' the top:* people in authority, although as prone to vice as others, use their authority as a cover and seem to be cured of their vice.
141-2. *She speaks . . . breeds with it:* Isabella's 'sense', i.e. her rational argument, kindles Angelo's 'sense', i.e. his sensuality.
144. *bethink me:* consider.

81

Isabella	Ay, with such gifts that heaven shall share with you.
Lucio	(*Aside to Isab*) You had marr'd all else.
Isabella	Not with fond sicles of the tested gold,
	Or stones whose rate are either rich or poor 150
	As fancy values them, but with true prayers
	That shall be up at heaven and enter there
	Ere sunrise: prayers from preserved souls,
	From fasting maids whose minds are dedicate
	To nothing temporal.
Angelo	Well: come to me tomorrow. 155
Lucio	(*Aside to Isab*) Go to; 'tis well; away.
Isabella	Heaven keep your honour safe!
Angelo	(*Aside*) Amen.
	For I am that way going to temptation,
	Where prayers cross.
Isabella	At what hour tomorrow
	Shall I attend your lordship?
Angelo	At any time 'fore noon. 160
Isabella	Save your honour!
	(*Exeunt Isabella, Lucio, and Provost*
Angelo	From thee—even from thy virtue!
	What's this? What's this? Is this her fault or mine?
	The tempter or the tempted, who sins most?
	Ha!
	Not she; nor doth she tempt: but it is I 165

148. *You had marr'd all else:* i.e. had you really meant 'bribe' you would have lost your cause.
149. *fond:* foolish. *sicles:* shekels. *tested:* refined.
150. *rate:* worth.
153. *preserved:* protected.
154. *fasting maids:* Isabella's fellow votarists.
155. *temporal:* worldly.
157. *your honour:* used by Isabella as a title of respect, but interpreted literally by Angelo.
158–9. *For . . . prayers cross:* for I am about to follow a line of temptation which goes counter to all prayers.
161. *Save:* God save.   *From thee:* said in answer to Isabella's parting prayer, 'God save you'.
165–8. *but it is I . . . virtuous season:* Angelo sees Isabella as the sun. Were he truly

That, lying by the violet in the sun,
Do as the carrion does, not as the flower,
Corrupt with virtuous season. Can it be
That modesty may more betray our sense
Than woman's lightness? Having waste ground
     enough,   170
Shall we desire to raze the sanctuary,
And pitch our evils there? O, fie, fie, fie!
What dost thou, or what art thou, Angelo?
Dost thou desire her foully for those things
That make her good? O, let her brother live: 175
Thieves for their robbery have authority,
When judges steal themselves. What, do I love
     her,
That I desire to hear her speak again,
And feast upon her eyes? What is't I dream on?
O cunning enemy, that, to catch a saint,   180
With saints dost bait thy hook! Most dangerous
Is that temptation that doth goad us on
To sin in loving virtue: never could the strumpet,
With all her double vigour, art and nature,
Once stir my temper; but this virtuous maid   185

---

virtuous, like the violet, her influence would preserve his virtue. However, the effect which she has upon him is like the sun's upon dead flesh: he is turned bad. For the Elizabethans the idea would have been even more powerful since they believed that the sun actually bred the maggots which were found in decayed flesh (cf. *Hamlet*, II, ii, 181).

167. *carrion:* dead flesh.

168. *Corrupt:* decay.   *season:* preservative.

168–70. *Can it be . . . woman's lightness:* can it be that chastity may be a greater temptation to sensuality than wantonness?

170–2. *Having . . . evils there:* since there is abundant waste land, why do I wish to destroy a temple and cast my filth there?

170. *waste ground:* i.e. the brothels.

171. *the sanctuary:* i.e. Isabella.

179–81. *What . . . hook:* Angelo imagines that he is a holy man being tempted in a dream by Satan disguised as a virgin saint.

182. *goad:* incite.

184. *her double vigour, art and nature:* her twofold power of attraction, skill and natural beauty.

185. *stir my temper:* disturb my composure.

Subdues me quite. Ever till now,
When men were fond, I smiled, and wonder'd how.

(*Exit*

Scene III. *The Prison*

Enter from opposite sides, Duke *disguised as a friar, and* Provost

Duke	Hail to you, provost—so I think you are.
Provost	I am the provost. What's your will, good friar?
Duke	Bound by my charity and my blest order,
	I come to visit the afflicted spirits
	Here in the prison. Do me the common right 5
	To let me see them, and to make me know
	The nature of their crimes, that I may minister
	To them accordingly.
Provost	I would do more than that, if more were needful.

Enter Juliet

Look, here comes one: a gentlewoman of mine,   10
Who, falling in the flaws of her own youth,
Hath blister'd her report. She is with child;
And he that got it, sentenced—a young man
More fit to do another such offence
Than die for this.   15

Duke	When must he die?
Provost	As I do think, tomorrow.
	(*To Juliet*) I have provided for you; stay a while,
	And you shall be conducted.
Duke	Repent you, fair one, of the sin you carry?

186. *subdues me quite:* overcomes me completely.
187. *fond:* infatuated.

3. *charity:* Christian love.
4. *afflicted spirits:* troubled souls.
5. *the common right:* i.e. the right given to holy men.
6. *make me know:* tell me.
11. *flaws:* passionate outbursts.
12. *blister'd her report:* tarnished her reputation.
19. *the sin you carry:* the sin which is manifest in your unborn child.

Juliet	I do; and bear the shame most patiently.	20
Duke	I'll teach you how you shall arraign your con-	
	science	
	And try your penitence, if it be sound,	
	Or hollowly put on.	
Juliet	I'll gladly learn.	
Duke	Love you the man that wrong'd you?	
Juliet	Yes, as I love the woman that wrong'd him.	25
Duke	So, then it seems your most offenceful act	
	Was mutually committed?	
Juliet	Mutually.	
Duke	Then was your sin of heavier kind than his.	
Juliet	I do confess it, and repent it, father.	
Duke	'Tis meet so, daughter, but lest you do repent,	30
	As that the sin hath brought you to this shame,	
	Which sorrow is always toward ourselves, not	
	heaven,	
	Showing we would not spare heaven as we love it,	
	But as we stand in fear—	
Juliet	I do repent me, as it is an evil,	35
	And take the shame with joy.	
Duke	There rest.	
	Your partner, as I hear, must die tomorrow,	
	And I am going with instruction to him.	
	Grace go with you, *Benedicite!* (*Exit*	
Juliet	Must die tomorrow! O injurious love,	40

21. *teach:* show. *arraign:* examine.
22–3. *if it be . . . put on:* if it be genuine or only a show.
25. *the woman that wrong'd him:* i.e. herself.
28. *Then . . . his:* the implication being that women have greater control over their passion than men have.
30–4. *but lest . . . stand in fear:* the Duke is distinguishing between two forms of penitence: self-pity effected through the shame of being found out, and genuine sorrow at having offended Heaven.
36. *There rest:* continue in that opinion.
39. *Benedicite:* bless you.
40–2. *injurious love . . . a dying horror:* Juliet's life has been spared because of the outcome of her love, i.e. her pregnancy. This consolation is 'injurious' since her life is spent contemplating the horror of Claudio's death.

That respites me a life, whose very comfort
Is still a dying horror!

Provost   'Tis pity of him.

                                       (*Exeunt*

Scene IV. *Angelo's House*

Enter Angelo

Angelo

When I would pray and think, I think and pray
To several subjects: Heaven hath my empty words,
Whilst my invention, hearing not my tongue,
Anchors on Isabel: God in my mouth,
As if I did but only chew his name,   5
And in my heart the strong and swelling evil
Of my conception. The state whereon I studied
Is like a good thing, being often read,
Grown sear'd and tedious: yea, my gravity,
Wherein—let no man hear me—I take pride,   10
Could I with boot change for an idle plume
Which the air beats for vain. O place, O form,
How often dost thou with thy case, thy habit,
Wrench awe from fools, and tie the wiser souls
To thy false seeming! Blood, thou art blood.   15

42. *'Tis pity of him:* he is to be pitied.

2. *several:* different.
3. *invention:* imagination.
4. *Anchors:* fixes.
7. *conception:* plan, design; but suggesting also 'original sin'. *The state whereon I studied:* the power on which my mind dwelled continually.
8. *read:* thought about.
9. *sear'd:* withered. *gravity:* seriousness.
11. *boot:* profit. *plume:* feather, emblem of frivolity.
12. *for vain:* for its vanity.
12–15. *O place . . . seeming:* how often do status and ceremony, with their external show, force fools to marvel at them and confine even the intelligent to their deceiving appearances.
15. *Blood, thou art blood:* Angelo finally acknowledges his sensual nature. Cf. I, iii, 52 and I, iv, 57–8.

Let's write 'good angel' on the devil's horn;
'Tis not the devil's crest.

Enter a Servant

                          How now? Who's there?

Servant   One Isabel, a sister, desires access to you.

Angelo   Teach her the way. (*Exit Servant*) O Heavens,
Why does my blood thus muster to my heart,   20
Making both it unable for itself
And dispossessing all my other parts
Of necessary fitness?
So play the foolish throngs with one that swoons,
Come all to help him, and so stop the air   25
By which he should revive; and even so
The general subject to a well-wish'd king
Quit their own part, and in obsequious fondness
Crowd to his presence, where their untaught love
Must needs appear offence.

Enter ISABELLA

                       How now, fair maid?   30

Isabella   I am come to know your pleasure.

16–17. *Let's write . . . devil's crest:* Angelo, as the Duke anticipated (I, iii, 52–4) has succumbed to temptation. He thinks of Isabella as a devil and wryly says that the devil's horn, thought to be his tell-tale emblem, should be stamped with a new emblem 'good angel'. Ironically the 'good' Angelo is himself about to take on the role of a devil.

18. *access:* admittance.

19. *Teach:* show.

20–30. *Why does my blood . . . appear offence:* the Elizabethans believed that in times of stress blood left the limbs and gathered round the heart. Angelo complains that both heart and limbs are incapacitated, and that the effect is similar to the well-intended stupidity of a crowd who gather round a person who has fainted, thus depriving him of air, and also to the equally well-intended offensiveness of people who flock around their King. (See also *Commentary 6*, 'The Duke and King James'.)

20. *muster:* gather.

27. *general subject:* common people.

28. *Quit their own part:* abandon their own role. *obsequious fondness:* foolish subservience.

29. *untaught:* ignorant.

31. *pleasure:* Angelo's reply takes up the sexual meaning.

Angelo	(*Aside*) That you might know it, would much better please me Than to demand what 'tis—Your brother cannot live.
Isabella	Even so. Heaven keep your honour!
Angelo	Yet may he live awhile; and, it may be, 35 As long as you or I: yet he must die.
Isabella	Under your sentence?
Angelo	Yea.
Isabella	When, I beseech you? That in his reprieve, Longer or shorter, he may be so fitted 40 That his soul sicken not.
Angelo	Ha! Fie, these filthy vices! It were as good To pardon him that hath from nature stolen A man already made, as to remit Their saucy sweetness that do coin heaven's image 45 In stamps that are forbid. 'Tis all as easy Falsely to take away a life true made, As to put metal in restrained means To make a false one.
Isabella	'Tis set down so in heaven, but not in earth. 50
Angelo	Say you so? Then I shall pose you quickly. Which had you rather, that the most just law Now took your brother's life; or, to redeem him, Give up your body to such sweet uncleanness As she that he hath stain'd?

34. *Even so:* so be it.
39. *reprieve:* time before execution.
40. *fitted:* prepared.
41. *That his soul sicken not:* that his soul may be untainted by earthly sin.
42–9. *It were . . . false one:* to pardon a man who has unlawfully made life would be the equivalent of pardoning a murderer, who has sinfully taken life. (Angelo proves consistent in the extremism of his morality. Believing that he has seduced Isabella, the 'murder' of Claudio is to him no worse an offence. (See also *Commentary 5*, 'Coining Images'.)
44. *remit:* pardon.
45. *saucy sweetness:* wanton self-indulgence.
47. *Falsely:* illegally.
48. *restrained means:* prohibited instruments.
51. *pose you:* put it to you.

Isabella	Sir, believe this, 55 I had rather give my body than my soul.
Angelo	I talk not of your soul: our compell'd sins Stand more for number than for accompt.
Isabella	How say you?
Angelo	Nay, I'll not warrant that: for I can speak Against the thing I say. Answer to this: 60 I, now the voice of the recorded law, Pronounce a sentence on your brother's life: Might there not be a charity in sin To save this brother's life?
Isabella	Please you to do't, I'll take it as a peril to my soul, 65 It is no sin at all, but charity.
Angelo	Pleased you to do't, at peril of your soul, Were equal poise of sin and charity.
Isabella	That I do beg his life, if it be sin, Heaven let me bear it; you granting of my suit, 70 If that be sin, I'll make it my morn prayer To have it added to the faults of mine, And nothing of your answer.
Angelo	Nay, but hear me; Your sense pursues not mine: either you are ignorant, Or seem so, crafty; and that's not good. 75
Isabella	Let me be ignorant, and in nothing good,

57–8. *our compell'd sins . . . accompt:* sins which we are forced to commit are
  recorded but do not weigh against us when we come to judgment.
59–60. *Nay . . . say:* I will not stand by that. It is my privilege as a judge to state
  something which I do not believe.
64. *Please you:* if you are willing.
67–8. *Pleased you . . . charity:* if you were to commit the sin which would save
  your brother's life the charity in the act would weigh equally with the sin.
69–70. *That I . . . bear it:* Isabella thinks that the sin in question is her pleading
  for her brother.
73. *nothing of your answer:* not added to the faults for which you will have to
  answer (when you die).
74. *sense:* again used ambiguously to mean both 'reason' and 'sensuality'; cf. II,
  ii, 142.

	But graciously to know I am no better.	
Angelo	Thus wisdom wishes to appear most bright	
	When it doth tax itself: as these black masks	
	Proclaim an enshield beauty ten times louder	80
	Than beauty could display'd. But mark me;	
	To be received plain, I'll speak more gross:	
	Your brother is to die.	
Isabella	So.	
Angelo	And his offence is so, as it appears,	85
	Accountant to the law upon that pain.	
Isabella	True.	
Angelo	Admit no other way to save his life—	
	As I subscribe not that, nor any other,	
	But in the loss of question—that you, his sister,	90
	Finding yourself desired of such a person,	
	Whose credit with the judge, or own great place,	
	Could fetch your brother from the manacles	
	Of the all-binding law; and that there were	
	No earthly mean to save him, but that either	95
	You must lay down the treasures of your body	
	To this supposed, or else to let him suffer:	
	What would you do?	
Isabella	As much for my poor brother as myself;	
	That is, were I under the terms of death,	100

77. *graciously:* through divine grace.
79: *tax:* accuse.   *these black masks:* Angelo may be alluding to the masks worn by
   some of the women in the audience, but it is possible that he may mean
   Isabella's habit or veil.
80. *enshield:* hidden.
82. *received plain:* clearly understood.   *gross:* obviously.
85. *so:* such.
86. *Accountant:* accountable.   *pain:* penalty.
89–90. *As I . . . question:* though I do not assent to the way which I am going to
   suggest, nor to any other, except hypothetically.
90. *the loss of question:* the absence of an actual issue.
92. *credit:* influence.   *place:* rank.
95. *mean:* way.
96. *the treasures of your body:* your virginity.
97. *this supposed:* this hypothethical person.
100. *terms:* sentence.

	Th'impression of keen whips I'd wear as rubies,	
	And strip myself to death as to a bed	
	That longing have been sick for, ere I'd yield	
	My body up to shame.	
Angelo	Then must your brother die.	
Isabella	And 'twere the cheaper way:	105

Angelo Then must your brother die.

Isabella And 'twere the cheaper way: 105
Better it were a brother died at once,
Than that a sister, by redeeming him,
Should die for ever.

Angelo Were not you then as cruel as the sentence
That you have slander'd so?   110

Isabella Ignomy in ransom and free pardon
Are of two houses: lawful mercy
Is nothing kin to foul redemption.

Angelo You seem'd of late to make the law a tyrant,
And rather proved the sliding of your brother   115
A merriment than a vice.

Isabella O pardon me, my lord; it oft falls out,
To have what we would have, we speak not what
    we mean:
I something do excuse the thing I hate,
For his advantage that I dearly love.   120

Angelo We are all frail.

Isabella   Else let my brother die,

100–4. *That is . . . My body up to shame:* see *Introduction*, pp. 17–18 (and cf. *Troilus and Cressida*, III, iii, 237–8, 'I have a woman's longing, An appetite that I am sick withal').

105. *cheaper:* easier.

106–8. *Better . . . ever:* it would be better for my brother to die now than for my soul to be lost eternally by my saving him.

110. *slander'd:* reproached.

111. *Ignomy:* ignominy, shame.

112. *Are of two houses:* are of different families, i.e. are completely different.

113. *nothing:* in no way.   *kin:* related.

115. *sliding:* moral slip.

119. *something:* to some extent.

121. *frail:* susceptible.

121–3. *Else . . . thy weakness:* if we were not all frail, and if Claudio's weakness was neither shared by others now nor to be inherited by later generations, then you could let him die.

	If not a feodary but only he	
	Owe and succeed thy weakness.	
Angelo	Nay, women are frail too.	
Isabella	Ay, as the glasses where they view themselves,	125

Which are as easy broke as they make forms.
Women! Help Heaven! Men their creation mar
In profiting by them. Nay, call us ten times frail;
For we are soft as our complexions are,
And credulous to false prints.

Angelo   I think it well: 130
And from this testimony of your own sex—
Since I suppose we are made to be no stronger
Than faults may shake our frames—let me be bold.
I do arrest your words. Be that you are,
That is, a woman; if you be more, you're none.   135
If you be one—as you are well express'd
By all external warrants—show it now,
By putting on the destined livery.

Isabella   I have no tongue but one; gentle my lord,
Let me entreat you speak the former language.   140

Angelo   Plainly conceive, I love you.

Isabella   My brother did love Juliet,
And you tell me that he shall die for't.

Angelo   He shall not, Isabel, if you give me love.

---

122. *feodary:* this word combines the meanings of 'accomplice' and 'feudal tenant'.
123. *Owe:* possess.   *succeed:* inherit.   *thy weakness:* the frailty which Angelo has just mentioned.
125. *glasses:* mirrors.
126. *make forms:* give reflections.
127–8. *Men . . . by them:* men (created in the likeness of God) impair their perfection by taking advantage of women.
130. *credulous to false prints:* 'easily seduced'. See *Commentary 5*, 'Coining Images'. *I think it well:* I agree.
132–3. *we are made . . . our frames:* we are made no stronger than the human weaknesses which beset our constitutions.
134. *I do arrest your words:* I will make you stand by what you have said.
136–7. *as you . . . warrants:* as you are shown to be by all external evidence.
138. *By putting on the destined livery:* i.e. by showing woman's characteristic weakness. *livery:* dress.
139. *tongue:* language.
141. *conceive:* understand.

Isabella	I know your virtue hath a licence in't, 145
	Which seems a little fouler than it is,
	To pluck on others.
Angelo	Believe me, on mine honour,
	My words express my purpose.
Isabella	Ha! Little honour to be much believed,
	And most pernicious purpose! Seeming, seeming! 150
	I will proclaim thee, Angelo, look for't.
	Sign me a present pardon for my brother,
	Or with an outstretch'd throat I'll tell the world
	aloud
	What man thou art.
Angelo	Who will believe thee, Isabel?
	My unsoil'd name, th'austereness of my life, 155
	My vouch against you, and my place i'th'state,
	Will so your accusation overweigh,
	That you shall stifle in your own report,
	And smell of calumny. I have begun,
	And now I give my sensual race the rein: 160
	Fit thy consent to my sharp appetite;
	Lay by all nicety and prolixious blushes
	That banish what they sue for: redeem thy
	brother
	By yielding up thy body to my will;
	Or else he must not only die the death, 165

145-7. *I know . . . others:* I know that your authority gives you a freedom which
    makes you appear worse than you really are in order to trap others.
150. *Seeming:* hypocrisy.
151. *proclaim thee:* denounce you publicly.
152. *present:* immediate.
156. *vouch:* testimony.
158-9. *That you shall . . . calumny:* that your account of what has happened will
    seem like slander, and you yourself will suffer.
160. *I give my sensual race the rein:* I give free play to my sensual nature.
161. *Fit:* adjust.   *sharp:* keen.
162-3. *Lay by . . . sue for:* put aside all coyness and time-wasting blushes which
    outwardly seem to banish the very desires which they excite.
163. *redeem:* save.
164. *will:* lust.

But thy unkindness shall his death draw out
To lingering sufferance. Answer me tomorrow,
Or, by the affection that now guides me most,
I'll prove a tyrant to him. As for you,
Say what you can, my false o'erweighs your true. 170
(*Exit*

Isabella   To whom should I complain? Did I tell this,
Who would believe me? O perilous mouths,
That bear in them one and the self-same tongue,
Either of condemnation or approof;
Bidding the law make curtsy to their will,   175
Hooking both right and wrong to th'appetite,
To follow as it draws! I'll to my brother:
Though he hath fall'n by prompture of the blood,
Yet hath he in him such a mind of honour,
That, had he twenty heads to tender down   180
On twenty bloody blocks, he'd yield them up
Before his sister should her body stoop
To such abhorr'd pollution.
Then, Isabel live chaste, and brother die:
More than our brother is our chastity.   185
I'll tell him yet of Angelo's request,
And fit his mind to death, for his soul's rest.
(*Exit*

---

166. *unkindness:* suggesting both 'cruelty' and 'lack of natural affection'.
167. *sufferance:* suffering.
168. *affection:* passion.
170. *my false o'erweighs your true:* my lies will be believed before your truths.
172–4. *O perilous mouths . . . or approof:* O cunning mouths that can with the same tongue speak for and against a cause.
175. *Bidding the law make curtsy to their will:* ordering the law to be subservient to their own lust.
176–7. *Hooking . . . draws:* making both right and wrong follow the dictates of sensual desire.
178. *prompture of the blood:* prompting of sensuality.
180. *tender:* pay.
182. *stoop:* submit.
187. *fit:* prepare.

ACT III

SCENE I. *A Prison Cell*

Enter DUKE *disguised as before,* CLAUDIO, *and* PROVOST

Duke	So then you hope of pardon from Lord Angelo?	
Claudio	The miserable have no other medicine	
	But only hope:	
	I have hope to live, and am prepared to die.	
Duke	Be absolute for death: either death or life	5

          Shall thereby be the sweeter. Reason thus with
             life:
          If I do lose thee, I do lose a thing
          That none but fools would keep: a breath thou art,
          Servile to all the skyey influences,
          That dost this habitation where thou keep'st   10
          Hourly afflict. Merely, thou art death's fool;
          For him thou labour'st by thy flight to shun,
          And yet run'st toward him still. Thou art not
             noble,
          For all th'accommodations that thou bear'st
          Are nursed by baseness. Thou'rt by no means
             valiant,   15
          For thou dost fear the soft and tender fork
          Of a poor worm. Thy best of rest is sleep,

5. *absolute:* positively decided.

8–11. *a breath . . . Hourly afflict:* 'You are a mere breath, subject to all the influences of the heavens, hourly afflicting (by your very existence) the world you live on.' *Dost* is 2nd. pers. sing., the antecedent of *that* (line 10) being *thou* (line 8). However, it is possible that *dost* is a printer's error for 'does' (a variant form of 'do' sometimes used by Shakespeare with a plural subject, which in this case would be *skyey influences*).

11–13. *Merely . . . run'st toward him still:* death makes an absolute fool of you: you try to run away from him, but all the time you are running toward him.

11. *Merely:* absolutely, entirely.

14–15. *For all th'accommodations . . . baseness:* for all the comforts of civilization which you produce are made out of base things. (Cf. *King Lear*, III, iv, 107–10.)

16. *fork:* i.e. forked tongue.

17. *worm:* snake.

95

And that thou oft provok'st, yet grossly fear'st
Thy death, which is no more. Thou art not thy-
    self,
For thou exists on many a thousand grains   20
That issue out of dust. Happy thou art not,
For what thou hast not, still thou striv'st to get,
And what thou hast, forget'st. Thou art not
    certain,
For thy complexion shifts to strange effects,
After the moon. If thou art rich, thou'rt poor,   25
For, like an ass whose back with ingots bows,
Thou bear'st thy heavy riches but a journey,
And death unloads thee. Friend hast thou none,
For thine own bowels, which do call thee sire,
The mere effusion of thy proper loins,   30
Do curse the gout, serpigo, and the rheum,
For ending thee no sooner. Thou hast nor youth
    nor age,
But as it were an after-dinner's sleep,
Dreaming on both; for all thy blessed youth
Becomes as agèd, and doth beg the alms   35
Of palsied eld; and when thou art old and rich,
Thou hast neither heat, affection, limb, nor beauty,
To make thy riches pleasant. What's yet in this

17–19. *Thy best of rest . . . no more:* you often induce sleep, the best form of rest, yet you have a great fear of death, which is only a form of sleep.

19–21. *Thou art not thyself . . . out of dust:* you have no real identity, for you are made of many tiny particles which come from dust.

23–5. *Thou art not certain . . . After the moon:* you are inconstant because your temperament is affected by the changes of the moon.

25. *poor:* unfortunate.

26. *ingots:* bars of precious metal.

29. *bowels:* offspring.

30. *mere:* pure, undiluted. *effusion:* issue. *proper:* own.

31. *serpigo:* a kind of skin disease. *rheum:* catarrh.

32. *nor . . . nor:* neither . . . nor.

34–6. *for all thy blessed youth . . . Of palsied eld:* because throughout the period when you are blessed with youth you act as though you were old and beg alms from trembling old age (just as old age begs 'arms' from youth).

37. *heat:* warmth. *affection:* passion. *limb:* denoting 'physical vigour'.

	That bears the name of life? Yet in this life	
	Lie hid moe thousand deaths; yet death we fear,	40
	That makes these odds all even.	
Claudio	I humbly thank you.	
	To sue to live, I find I seek to die,	
	And seeking death, find life. Let it come on.	
Isabella	(*within*) What, ho! Peace here; grace and good company!	
Provost	Who's there? Come in; the wish deserves a welcome.	45
Duke	Dear sir, ere long I'll visit you again.	
Claudio	Most holy sir, I thank you.	

Enter ISABELLA

Isabella	My business is a word or two with Claudio.	
Provost	And very welcome. Look signior, here's your sister.	50
Duke	Provost, a word with you.	
Provost	As many as you please.	
Duke	Bring me to hear them speak, where I may be concealed.	

(Exeunt Duke and Provost

Claudio	Now, sister, what's the comfort?	55
Isabella	Why,	
	As all comforts are: most good, most good indeed.	
	Lord Angelo, having affairs to heaven,	
	Intends you for his swift ambassador,	
	Where you shall be an everlasting leiger.	60

38–9. *What's yet . . . name of life:* 'What is there in such a state of affairs as *this* that can be worth calling "life"?'
40. *moe thousand:* a thousand more.
41. *That makes these odds all even:* that cancels out these calamities.
42. *To sue . . . to die:* in begging to live I find that I wish to die.
43. *life:* i.e. eternal life.
58. *having affairs to heaven:* having business in heaven.
60. *leiger:* representative, agent.

	Therefore your best appointment make with speed:	
	Tomorrow you set on.	
Claudio	Is there no remedy?	
Isabella	None but such remedy as, to save a head,	
	To cleave a heart in twain.	
Claudio	But is there any?	
Isabella	Yes, brother, you may live;	65
	There is a devilish mercy in the judge,	
	If you'll implore it, that will free your life,	
	But fetter you till death.	
Claudio	Perpetual durance?	
Isabella	Ay, just, perpetual durance; a restraint,	
	Though all the world's vastidity you had,	70
	To a determined scope.	
Claudio	But in what nature?	
Isabella	In such a one as, you consenting to't,	
	Would bark your honour from that trunk you bear,	
	And leave you naked.	
Claudio.	Let me know the point.	
Isabella	O, I do fear thee, Claudio, and I quake	75
	Lest thou a feverous life shouldst entertain,	
	And six or seven winters more respect	

61. *appointment:* preparation.
62. *set on:* start, i.e. die.   *remedy:* way out.
63–4. *None . . . To cleave a heart in twain:* no remedy, apart from one which in saving (your) life would break (my) heart.
68. *Perpetual durance:* life imprisonment.
69. *Ay, just:* exactly.
69–71. *a restraint . . . To a determined scope:* a form of imprisonment which would confine you even though you were given all the freedom this earthly life offers.
70. *vastidity:* vastness.
71. *determined scope:* limited freedom.   *nature:* way.
72–4. *In such a one . . . leave you naked:* in such a way that, were you to consent to it, you would be stripped of all your honour.
73. *trunk:* i.e. body.
75. *quake:* tremble.
76. *feverous:* feverish.   *entertain:* keep up, maintain.
77. *respect:* consider, regard.

	Than a perpetual honour. Dar'st thou die?	
	The sense of death is most in apprehension;	
	And the poor beetle that we tread upon,	80
	In corporal sufferance finds a pang as great	
	As when a giant dies.	

Claudio
                          Why give you me this shame?
Think you I can a resolution fetch
From flowery tenderness? If I must die,
I will encounter darkness as a bride   85
And hug it in mine arms.

Isabella
There spake my brother, there my father's grave
Did utter forth a voice. Yes, thou must die.
Thou art too noble to conserve a life
In base appliances. This outward-sainted deputy,   90
Whose settled visage and deliberate word
Nips youth i' th'head, and follies doth enew
As falcon doth the fowl, is yet a devil:
His filth within being cast, he would appear
A pond as deep as hell.

Claudio
                          The prenzie Angelo?   95

Isabella
O, 'tis the cunning livery of hell,
The damned'st body to invest and cover
In prenzie guards. Dost thou think, Claudio,
If I would yield him my virginity
Thou mightst be freed.

79. *sense:* feeling, pain. *apprehension:* imagination.
81. *corporal sufferance:* physical suffering.
83–4. *Think you . . . From flowery tenderness:* do you think that your sentimental
    eloquence can help me to find courage?
87–8. *my father's grave . . . a voice:* my dead father spoke from within you.
90. *appliances:* remedies.
91. *settled visage:* composed face. *deliberate word:* well-weighed speech.
92. *Nips youth i'th'head:* kills youth: birds of prey kill their quarry in this way
    (cf. II, i, 2). *follies:* wantonness. *enew:* drive into hiding; a term used in
    falconry.
94. *cast:* thrown up.
95, 98. *prenzie:* a word which may be a printer's error; it has been suggested
    that it means 'princely' or that it may be a misreading of 'precise'.
96. *livery:* uniform.
97. *invest:* adorn.
98. *guards:* trimmings.

Claudio	O heavens, it cannot be! 100
Isabella	Yes, he would give't thee, from this rank offence,
	So to offend him still. This night's the time
	That I should do what I abhor to name,
	Or else thou diest tomorrow.
Claudio	Thou shalt not do't.
Isabella	O, were it but my life, 105
	I'd throw it down for your deliverance
	As frankly as a pin.
Claudio	Thanks, dear Isabel.
Isabella	Be ready, Claudio, for your death tomorrow.
Claudio	Yes. Has he affections in him,
	That thus can make him bite the law by th'nose 110
	When he would force it? Sure, it is no sin;
	Or of the deadly seven it is the least.
Isabella	Which is the least?
Claudio	If it were damnable, he being so wise,
	Why would he for the momentary trick 115
	Be perdurably fined? O Isabel!
Isabella	What says my brother?
Claudio	Death is a fearful thing.
Isabella	And shamèd life a hateful.
Claudio	Ay, but to die, and go we know not where;
	To lie in cold obstruction and to rot; 120
	This sensible warm motion to become
	A kneaded clod; and the delighted spirit

101-2. *he would . . . offend him still:* in return for this foul offence of mine he would let you live on to offend again. (Isabella is making use of one of Angelo's arguments for Claudio's death; cf. II, ii, 103-4.)

107. *frankly:* freely.

109. *affections:* passions.

110. *bite the law by th'nose:* mock the law.

111. *would force it:* wishes to enforce the law. *it is no sin:* i.e. lechery is no sin.

115. *momentary trick:* passing game.

116. *perdurably fined:* everlastingly punished.

120. *cold obstruction:* a term used for the cessation of the vital functions in death. In juxtaposition to 'sensible warm motion' it suggests the pressing down of cold earth on a still living body.

121-2. *This sensible . . . A kneaded clod:* the power of movement, warm and able to feel sensation, to become compressed into earth.

To bathe in fiery floods, or to reside
In thrilling region of thick-ribbed ice;
To be imprison'd in the viewless winds   125
And blown with restless violence round about
The pendent world; or to be worse than worst
Of those that lawless and incertain thought
Imagine howling—'tis too horrible.
The weariest and most loathèd worldly life   130
That age, ache, penury, and imprisonment
Can lay on nature is a paradise
To what we fear of death.

Isabella   Alas, alas!

Claudio   Sweet sister, let me live.
What sin you do to save a brother's life,   135
Nature dispenses with the deed so far
That it becomes a virtue.

Isabella   O you beast!
O faithless coward! O dishonest wretch!
Wilt thou be made a man out of my vice?
Is't not a kind of incest, to take life   140
From thine own sister's shame? What should I
    think?
Heaven shield my mother play'd my father fair:
For such a warped slip of wilderness
Ne'er issued from his blood. Take my defiance!

122. *delighted spirit:* animated life force.
123, 124. *fiery floods, thick-ribbed ice:* the elemental extremes characteristic of hell.
124. *thrilling:* piercing.
125. *viewless:* invisible.
127. *pendent:* hanging unsupported in space.
127–9. *or to be . . . Imagine howling:* or to suffer more horribly than the most tormented soul in a hell imagined by unrestrained and chaotic minds.
131. *penury:* poverty.
132. *Can lay on nature:* can inflict on human nature.
136. *dispenses with:* pardons.
140–1. *Is't not . . . own sister's shame:* would it not be a kind of incest for you to be given life as a result of my being seduced?
142. *Heaven shield . . . fair:* Heaven forbid that my mother stayed faithful to my father, i.e. that you are my father's son.
143. *warped:* perverse, malignant. *slip:* scion, offshoot. *of wilderness:* barren, worthless.

	Die, perish! Might but my bending down 145
	Reprieve thee from thy fate, it should proceed.
	I'll pray a thousand prayers for thy death,
	No word to save thee.
Claudio	Nay hear me, Isabel—
Isabella	O fie, fie, fie!
	Thy sin's not accidental, but a trade! 150
	Mercy to thee would prove itself a bawd;
	'Tis best that thou diest quickly.
Claudio	O, hear me, Isabella—

Re-enter DUKE

Duke	Vouchsafe a word, young sister, but one word.
Isabella	What is your will?
Duke	Might you dispense with your leisure, I would 155 by and by have some speech with you: the satisfaction I would require is likewise your own benefit.
Isabella	I have no superfluous leisure; my stay must be stolen out of other affairs; but I will attend you 160 awhile.
	(*Walks apart*
Duke	Son, I have overheard what hath passed between you and your sister. Angelo had never the purpose to corrupt her; only he hath made an assay of her virtue to practise his judgement with the dis- 165 position of natures. She, having the truth of

150. *Thy sin's . . . a trade:* your sin was not an isolated incident but an habitual practice.
151. *Mercy . . . a bawd:* granting you your life would give an incentive to prostitution.
153. *Vouchsafe:* grant me.
155. *dispense with:* do without.
156. *by and by:* soon.
156–8. *the satisfaction . . . benefit:* by granting my request you too will benefit.
160. *attend you:* listen to you.
164. *assay:* test.
165–6. *to practise . . . of natures:* to obtain skill in judging different types of human nature.

	honour in her, hath made him that gracious denial which he is most glad to receive. I am confessor to Angelo, and I know this to be true; therefore prepare yourself to death: do not satisfy your 170 resolution with hopes that are fallible. Tomorrow you must die; go to your knees, and make ready.
Claudio	Let me ask my sister pardon. I am so out of love with life, that I will sue to be rid of it.
Duke	Hold you there: farewell. (*Exit Claudio*) Provost, 175 a word with you!

Re-enter PROVOST

Provost	What's your will, father?
Duke	That now you are come, you will be gone. Leave me awhile with the maid; my mind promises with my habit no loss shall touch her by 180 my company.
Provost	In good time.

(*Exit Provost. Isabella comes forward*

| Duke | The hand that hath made you fair hath made you good; the goodness that is cheap in beauty makes beauty brief in goodness; but grace, being the 185 soul of your complexion, shall keep the body of it ever fair. The assault that Angelo hath made to you, fortune hath conveyed to my understanding; |

170–1. *do not satisfy . . . fallible:* do not replace your determination to face death with the temporary satisfaction of hopes which may be false.

174. *sue:* beg.

175. *Hold you there:* remain in that frame of mind.

179–81. *my mind promises . . . company:* both my mind and my dress are a guarantee that no harm will come to her if she is left with me.

182. *In good time:* right away.

184–5. *the goodness . . . in goodness:* the physical excellence which is so easily achieved by the beautiful results in their having little moral excellence.

185–7. *but grace . . . ever fair:* but your beauty has resulted from spiritual goodness and will last forever.

187. *assault:* sexual advance.

188. *fortune . . . my understanding:* I heard about by chance.

and, but that frailty hath examples for his falling,
I should wonder at Angelo. How will you do 190
to content this substitute, and to save your
brother?

Isabella I am now going to resolve him: I had rather my
brother die by the law than my son should be
unlawfully born. But O, how much is the good 195
Duke deceived in Angelo! If ever he return and
I can speak to him, I will open my lips in vain, or
discover his government.

Duke That shall not be much amiss; yet, as the matter
now stands, he will avoid your accusation—he 200
made trial of you only. Therefore fasten your ear
on my advisings; to the love I have in doing good
a remedy presents itself. I do make myself believe
that you may most uprighteously do a poor
wronged lady a merited benefit; redeem your 205
brother from the angry law; do no stain to your
own gracious person; and much please the absent
Duke, if peradventure he shall ever return to have
hearing of this business.

Isabella Let me hear you speak farther. I have spirit to 210
do any thing that appears not foul in the truth of
my spirit.

189. *but that frailty . . . falling:* were there not other examples of similar human
weakness.
191. *content:* satisfy.   *this substitute:* this deputy, i.e. Angelo.
193. *resolve him:* give him a definite answer.
198. *discover:* expose.   *government:* conduct, way in which he has governed.
200. *avoid:* refute.
200-1. *he made trial of you only:* i.e. by saying that his attempted seduction was only
meant to test Isabella.
202. *advisings:* advice.
203. *I do . . . believe:* I believe.
204. *uprighteously:* righteously, with integrity.
206. *stain:* disgrace.
208. *peradventure:* by chance.
210-12. *I have spirit . . . my spirit:* I am willing to do anything which does not
seem to be sinful to my conscience.

Duke	Virtue is bold, and goodness never fearful. Have you not heard speak of Mariana, the sister of Frederick, the great soldier who miscarried at sea? 215
Isabella	I have heard of the lady, and good words went with her name.
Duke	She should this Angelo have married; was affianced to her by oath, and the nuptial appointed: between which time of the contract and limit of 220 the solemnity, her brother Frederick was wrecked at sea, having in that perished vessel the dowry of his sister. But mark how heavily this befell to the poor gentlewoman. There she lost a noble and renowned brother, in his love toward her ever 225 most kind and natural; with him, the portion and sinew of her fortune, her marriage-dowry; with both, her combinate husband, this well-seeming Angelo.
Isabella	Can this be so? Did Angelo so leave her? 230
Duke	Left her in her tears, and dried not one of them with his comfort; swallowed his vows whole, pretending in her discoveries of dishonour: in few, bestowed her on her own lamentation, which she yet wears for his sake; and he, a marble to her 235 tears, is washed with them, but relents not.
Isabella	What a merit were it in death to take this poor

218–23. *She should . . . his sister:* see *Commentary 10*, 'Elizabethan Marriage Contracts'.
218–19. *was affianced:* sc. *he* was betrothed.   *nuptial:* wedding.
220–1. *between . . . solemnity:* between the time of the betrothal and the wedding ceremony.
223–4. *But mark . . . gentlewoman:* but listen to the sad effect which this had on Mariana.
227. *sinew:* mainstay.
228. *combinate:* betrothed.
233. *pretending . . . dishonour:* pretending to have discovered that she was not chaste.
233. *in few:* in short.
234. *bestowed her on her own lamentation:* left her with her grief.
235. *a marble:* i.e. cold and impervious as stone.

maid from the world! What corruption in this
life, that it will let this man live! But how out of
this can she avail? 240

Duke It is a rupture that you may easily heal: and the
cure of it not only saves your brother, but keeps
you from dishonour in doing it.

Isabella Show me how, good father.

Duke This forenamed maid hath yet in her the continu- 245
ance of her first affection. His unjust unkindness,
that in all reason should have quenched her love,
hath, like an impediment in the current, made it
more violent and unruly. Go you to Angelo;
answer his requiring with a plausible obedience; 250
agree with his demands to the point. Only refer
yourself to this advantage, first, that your stay
with him may not be long; that the time may
have all shadow and silence in it; and the place
answer to convenience. This being granted in 255
course, and now follows all. We shall advise this
wronged maid to stead up your appointment, go
in your place; if the encounter acknowledge itself
hereafter, it may compel him to her recompense.
And here, by this, is your brother saved, your 260
honour untainted, the poor Mariana advantaged,
and the corrupt Deputy scaled. The maid will I

240. *avail:* benefit.
241. *rupture:* breach.
242. *cure of it:* remedy.
245–6. *hath yet . . . affection:* still loves Angelo.
250. *answer . . . plausible obedience:* pretend to agree to his request.
251. *to the point:* exactly.
251–2. *refer yourself to this advantage:* place your reliance on this arrangement.
253–4. *that the time . . . silence in it:* i.e. that the encounter be in the middle of the
night.
254–5. *and the place answer to convenience:* that the place be convenient.
255–6. *in course:* as a matter of course.
257. *to stead up your appointment:* to stand in for you at the encounter.
258–9. *if the encounter . . . recompense:* if it is later discovered that they have had
this meeting (the implication being that Mariana may become pregnant) he
may be forced to make compensation to her.
262. *scaled:* weighed up.

frame and make fit for his attempt. If you think
well to carry this, as you may, the doubleness of
the benefit defends the deceit from reproof. What 265
think you of it?

Isabella The image of it gives me content already and I
trust it will grow to a most prosperous perfection.

Duke It lies much in your holding up. Haste you
speedily to Angelo. If for this night he entreat 270
you to his bed, give him promise of satisfaction.
I will presently to Saint Luke's; there at the
moated grange resides this dejected Mariana. At
that place call upon me; and dispatch with Angelo,
that it may be quickly. 275

Isabella I thank you for this comfort. Fare you well, good
father.

(Exeunt severally

SCENE II. *The street before the prison*

Enter, on one side, DUKE *disguised as before; on the other,* ELBOW,
and Officers *with* POMPEY

Elbow Nay, if there be no remedy for it, but that you
will needs buy and sell men and women like
beasts, we shall have all the world drink brown and
white bastard.

263. *frame:* prepare. *fit:* ready.
264. *carry this, as you may:* undertake to do this as best you can.
264–5. *the doubleness of the benefit:* i.e. the advantage to both you and Mariana.
265. *defends the deceit from reproof:* vindicates the deception from censure.
267. *image:* idea.
268. *perfection:* execution, completion.
269. *holding up:* carrying it out.
272. *presently:* at once.
274. *dispatch:* settle things promptly.

3–4. *drink brown and white bastard:* produce a variety of illegitimate children.
Elbow's pun hinges on the word 'bastard', which was also a type of Spanish
wine.

Duke	O heavens, what stuff is here?	5
Pompey	'Twas never merry world since, of two usuries,	
	the merriest was put down, and the worser allowed	
	by order of law; a furred gown to keep him	
	warm; and furred with fox and lambskins too,	
	to signify that craft, being richer than innocency,	10
	stands for the facing.	
Elbow	Come your way, sir. Bless you, good father	
	friar.	
Duke	And you, good brother father. What offence	
	hath this man made you, sir?	15
Elbow	Marry, sir, he hath offended the law; and, sir, we	
	take him to be a thief too, sir: for we have found	
	upon him, sir, a strange pick-lock which we have	
	sent to the deputy.	
Duke	Fie, sirrah, a bawd, a wicked bawd;	20
	The evil that thou causest to be done,	
	That is thy means to live. Do thou but think	
	What 'tis to cram a maw or clothe a back	
	From such a filthy vice: say to thyself,	
	From their abominable and beastly touches	25
	I drink, I eat, array myself, and live.	

6. *two usuries:* the 'merriest', prostitution; the 'worser', money lending.

7. *put down:* prohibited.

8. *by order of law:* a statute of 1571 allowed money lending at a rate of ten per cent.

8. *furred gown:* there are numerous references in Elizabethan literature to usurers dressed in fox furs.

9–11. *and furred . . . the facing:* the usurer's gown was made of lambskin trimmed with fox fur. Pompey suggests that the design of the gown was emblematic: the 'fox' standing for 'craft' being richer than 'lamb' representing 'innocence'.

11. *facing:* trimming.

13. *friar:* friar means, of course, 'brother', hence the Duke's retort.

18. *a strange pick-lock:* probably a reference to an instrument used to unlock 'chastity-belts'. It would, of course, be ironic that the instrument should be sent to Angelo, himself engaged in trying to pick the lock of Isabella's chastity.

20. *sirrah:* a form of address for inferiors.

23. *cram a maw:* fill a belly.

25. *touches:* sexual contacts.

26. *array:* dress.

	Canst thou believe thy living is a life, So stinkingly depending? Go mend, go mend.	
Pompey	Indeed, it does stink in some sort, sir; but yet, sir, I would prove—	30
Duke	Nay, if the devil have given thee proofs for sin, Thou wilt prove his. Take him to prison, officer: Correction and instruction must both work Ere this rude beast will profit.	
Elbow	He must before the deputy, sir; he has given him warning. The deputy cannot abide a whore- master: if he be a whoremonger, and comes before him, he were as good go a mile on his errand.	35
Duke	That we were all, as some would seem to be, From our faults, as faults from seeming, free!	40
Elbow	His neck will come to your waist—a cord, sir.	
Pompey	I spy comfort; I cry bail. Here's a gentleman and a friend of mine.	

Enter LUCIO

Lucio	How now, noble Pompey! What, at the wheels of Caesar? Art thou led in triumph? What, is there none of Pygmalion's images, newly made	45

27-8. *Canst . . . depending:* Can you call your existence 'life' when it depends on something so disgusting?

28. *mend:* reform.

29. *sort:* way.

31-2. *if the devil . . . prove his:* if the devil has given you arguments to defend sin you will be damned.

36. *whoremaster:* bawd.

37. *whoremonger:* fornicator.

38-9. *he were . . . errand:* a proverb meaning 'anything would be preferable'.

40-1. *That we were all . . . from seeming, free:* would that we were all, as some seem to be, as free from sin as sin is free from false-seeming. The Duke is contrasting Angelo 'the seemer' with Pompey 'the sinner'.

42. *His neck . . . a cord, sir:* his neck, like your waist, will soon have a cord round it.

46. *Caesar:* cf. II, i, 249.

46-9. *is there none . . . clutched:* are there no more whores to be bought? Pygmalion was a mythical figure who made a statue which came to life. The comparison between statues and whores was based on the fact that in Elizabethan England statues, like whores, were often painted.

	woman, to be had now, for putting the hand in the pocket and extracting clutched? What reply, ha? What say'st thou to this tune, matter and 50 method? Is't not drowned i' th'last rain, ha? What say'st thou, trot? Is the world as it was, man? Which is the way? Is it sad, and few words? Or how? The trick of it?
Duke	Still thus, and thus; still worse! 55
Lucio	How doth my dear morsel, thy mistress? Procures she still, ha?
Pompey	Troth, sir, she hath eaten up all her beef, and she is herself in the tub.
Lucio	Why, 'tis good! It is the right of it: it must be 60 so. Ever your fresh whore and your powdered bawd; an unshunned consequence; it must be so. Art going to prison, Pompey?
Pompey	Yes, faith, sir.
Lucio	Why, 'tis not amiss, Pompey. Farewell: go say I 65 sent thee thither. For debt, Pompey, or how?
Elbow	For being a bawd, for being a bawd.
Lucio	Well, then, imprison him: if imprisonment be the due of a bawd, why, 'tis his right. Bawd is he doubtless, and of antiquity too; bawd-born. 70

50–1. *What say'st . . . method:* what do you think of this new state of affairs?
51. *Is't not drowned:* is not prostitution completely wiped out?   *i' th' last rain:* this may be a topical allusion to the floods of 1602–3.
52. *trot:* a term of contempt, usually used of a midwife or other old woman.
54. *trick:* way.
56. *morsel:* a slang term for woman.
56–7. *Procures she still:* does she still obtain women to become prostitutes?
58–9. *she hath eaten . . . tub:* 'She has no more prostitutes and is taking a cure for venereal disease.' The Elizabethans cured meat by salting it; venereal disease was cured by putting the patient in a sulphur bath. 'Beef' was a slang term for prostitute.
61–2. *Ever . . . unshunned consequence:* the inexperienced young whore must inevitably become a painted and disease-ridden procuress. 'Powdering' was a term given to salting beef; cf. ll. 58–9, n.
62. *unshunned:* unavoidable.
65–6. *say I sent thee thither:* perhaps confirming Mistress Overdone's accusation that Lucio has acted as an informer, l. 201.
70. *of antiquity too:* of long standing.   *bawd-born:* i.e. his mother was a bawd.

	Farewell, good Pompey. Commend me to the prison, Pompey; you will turn good husband now, Pompey; you will keep the house.	
Pompey	I hope, sir, your good worship will be my bail?	
Lucio	No, indeed, will I not, Pompey; it is not the wear. I will pray, Pompey, to increase your bondage; if you take it not patiently, why, your mettle is the more. Adieu, trusty Pompey. Bless you, friar.	75
Duke	And you.	80
Lucio	Does Bridget paint still, Pompey, ha?	
Elbow	Come your ways, sir; come.	
Pompey	You will not bail me, then, sir?	
Lucio	Then, Pompey, nor now. What news abroad, friar? What news?	85
Elbow	Come your ways, sir, come.	
Lucio	Go to kennel, Pompey, go. (*Exeunt Elbow, Pompey and Officers*) What news, friar, of the Duke?	
Duke	I know none: can you tell me of any?	
Lucio	Some say he is with the Emperor of Russia; other some, he is in Rome: but where is he, think you?	90
Duke	I know not where: but wheresoever, I wish him well.	
Lucio	It was a mad fantastical trick of him to steal from the state, and usurp the beggary he was never born to. Lord Angelo dukes it well in his absence: he	95

71. *Commend:* remember.
73. *keep the house:* stay at home.
75–6. *the wear:* the fashion.
78. *mettle:* a pun on 'mettle' meaning 'spirit' and 'metal' referring to the chains with which Pompey is bound.
81. *paint:* use cosmetics.
84. *abroad:* in the world.
87. *kennel:* i.e. prison.
94. *fantastical:* fanciful, capricious.
94–5. *to steal from the state:* to leave the state secretively.
95. *usurp the beggary:* to take on the role of a beggar. (This is a joke at 'the Friar's' expense since the *audience* know that he is the Duke in disguise.)
96. *dukes it:* plays the duke.

	puts transgression to't.
Duke	He does well in't.
Lucio	A little more lenity to lechery would do no harm
	in him: something too crabbed that way, friar. 100
Duke	It is too general a vice, and severity must cure it.
Lucio	Yes, in good sooth, the vice is of a great kindred;
	it is well allied; but it is impossible to extirp it
	quite, friar, till eating and drinking be put down.
	They say this Angelo was not made by man and 105
	woman, after this downright way of creation: is it
	true, think you?
Duke	How should he be made, then?
Lucio	Some report a sea-maid spawned him; some that
	he was begot between two stock-fishes. But it is 110
	certain that when he makes water, his urine is
	congealed ice; that I know to be true. And he is
	a motion generative; that's infallible.
Duke	You are pleasant, sir, and speak apace.
Lucio	Why, what a ruthless thing is this in him, for the 115
	rebellion of a codpiece to take away the life of a
	man! Would the Duke that is absent have done
	this? Ere he would have hanged a man for the
	getting a hundred bastards, he would have paid for
	the nursing a thousand! He had some feeling of 120

96–7. *puts transgression to't:* has taken extreme measures against wrongdoing.
100. *something too crabbed:* rather too harsh.
102. *in good sooth:* truly.
102. *is of a great kindred:* has many relations.
103. *allied:* connected, related. *extirp:* root out.
104. *put down:* abolished.
106. *downright:* straightforward.
109. *sea-maid:* mermaid.
110. *stock-fishes:* dried codfishes (suggesting a lack of sexual appetite).
112–13. *And he . . . that's infallible:* it is certain that he has the sexual potency of a puppet ('motion').
114. *pleasant:* merry. *apace:* very freely.
115. *ruthless:* merciless.
116. *the rebellion of a codpiece:* i.e. an act of fornication. (The codpiece was an attachment worn on the front of the breeches, often very conspicuous in Elizabethan dress.)
120. *feeling:* experience.

	the sport; he knew the service; and that instructed	
	him to mercy.	
Duke	I never heard the absent Duke much detected for	
	women; he was not inclined that way.	
Lucio	O sir, you are deceived.	125
Duke	'Tis not possible.	
Lucio	Who, not the Duke? Yes, your beggar of fifty;	
	and his use was to put a ducat in her clack-dish!	
	The Duke had crotchets in him. He would be	
	drunk too, that let me inform you.	130
Duke	You do him wrong, surely.	
Lucio	Sir, I was an inward of his. A shy fellow was the	
	Duke; and I believe I know the cause of his with-	
	drawing.	
Duke	What, I prithee, might be the cause?	135
Lucio	No, pardon: 'tis a secret must be locked within	
	the teeth and the lips. But this I can let you	
	understand: the greater file of the subject held	
	the Duke to be wise.	
Duke	Wise! Why, no question but he was.	140
Lucio	A very superficial, ignorant, unweighing fellow.	
Duke	Either this is envy in you, folly, or mistaking: the	
	very stream of his life and the business he hath	
	helmed must, upon a warranted need, give him a	
	better proclamation. Let him be but testimonied	145
	in his own bringings-forth, and he shall appear to	
	the envious a scholar, a statesman and a soldier.	

121. *the sport:* lechery. *the service:* the profession, i.e. prostitution. *instructed:* trained.
123. *detected:* found out.
128. *use:* custom. *ducat:* a gold coin. *clack-dish:* begging-dish.
129. *crotchets:* perverse ideas.
132. *inward:* intimate friend.
138. *the greater file of the subject:* the majority of the people.
141. *unweighing:* thoughtless.
143. *stream:* passage.
144. *helmed:* steered. *upon a warranted need:* if proof were required.
145. *proclamation:* reputation.
145–6. *Let him . . . bringings-forth:* let his own achievements testify for him.
147. *envious:* malicious, spiteful.

	Therefore you speak unskilfully; or if your knowledge be more, it is much darkened in your malice. 150
Lucio	Sir, I know him, and I love him.
Duke	Love talks with better knowledge, and knowledge with dearer love.
Lucio	Come, sir, I know what I know.
Duke	I can hardly believe that, since you know not what 155 you speak. But, if ever the Duke return, as our prayers are he may, let me desire you to make your answer before him. If it be honest you have spoke, you have courage to maintain it: I am bound to call upon you; and, I pray you, your 160 name?
Lucio	Sir, my name is Lucio, well known to the Duke.
Duke	He shall know you better, sir, if I may live to report you.
Lucio	I fear you not. 165
Duke	O, you hope the Duke will return no more; or you imagine me too unhurtful an opposite. But indeed, I can do you little harm; you'll forswear this again.
Lucio	I'll be hanged first: thou art deceived in me, friar. 170 But no more of this. Canst thou tell if Claudio die tomorrow or no?
Duke	Why should he die, sir?
Lucio	Why? For filling a bottle with a tun-dish. I would the Duke we talk of were returned again: 175 this ungenitured agent will unpeople the province with continency. Sparrows must not build in his

148. *unskilfully:* ignorantly.
157–8. *to make your answer:* to defend yourself.
167. *unhurtful:* harmless. *opposite:* opponent.
168. *forswear:* deny.
174. *For . . . tun-dish:* for a mere act of fornication. *tun-dish:* funnel.
176. *this ungenitured agent:* this impotent deputy.
177. *continency:* chastity.

house-eaves, because they are lecherous. The
Duke yet would have dark deeds darkly answered;
he would never bring them to light: would he 180
were returned! Marry, this Claudio is condemned
for untrussing. Farewell, good friar. I prithee,
pray for me. The Duke, I say to thee again,
would eat mutton on Fridays. He's now past it,
yet, and I say to thee, he would mouth with a 185
beggar, though she smelt brown bread and garlic:
say that I said so. Farewell.   (*Exit*

Duke   No might nor greatness in mortality
Can censure 'scape; back-wounding calumny
The whitest virtue strikes. What king so strong 190
Can tie the gall up in the slanderous tongue?
But who comes here?

Enter ESCALUS, PROVOST, *and* Officers *with* MISTRESS
OVERDONE

Escalus   Go, away with her to prison!

Mistr. Overdone Good my lord, be good to me! Your honour is
accounted a merciful man; good my lord.   195

Escalus   Double and treble admonition, and still forfeit in
the same kind! This would make mercy swear
and play the tyrant.

Provost   A bawd of eleven years' continuance, may it
please your honour.   200

Mistr. Overdone My lord, this is one Lucio's information against

179. *darkly answered:* kept secret.
181. *Marry:* indeed.
182. *untrussing:* undoing his breeches.
184. *would eat mutton on Fridays:* would break the law of abstinence, i.e. would sin.
    There is also a pun on the slang meaning of 'mutton', a prostitute.
184. *He's now past it:* he's too old to perform the sexual act.
185. *mouth:* kiss.
186. *smelt:* smelt of.
188. *mortality:* human life.
189. *Can censure 'scape:* can escape hostile criticism.   *back-wounding:* wounding
    treacherously from behind.
191. *gall:* spite, bitterness.
196. *admonition:* warning.
196–7. *and still . . . kind:* and still guilty of offending in the same way.

me. Mistress Kate Keepdown was with child by
him in the Duke's time; he promised her marriage; his child is a year and a quarter old, come
Philip and Jacob: I have kept it myself; and see 205
how he goes about to abuse me!

Escalus   That fellow is a fellow of much licence: let him
be called before us. Away with her to prison. Go
to, no more words. (*Exeunt Officers with Mistress
Ov.*) Provost, my brother Angelo will not be 210
altered; Claudio must die tomorrow. Let him be
furnished with divines, and have all charitable
preparation. If my brother wrought by my pity,
it should not be so with him.

Provost   So please you, this friar hath been with him, and 215
advised him for th'entertainment of death.

Escalus   Good even, good father.

Duke   Bliss and goodness on you!

Escalus   Of whence are you?

Duke   Not of this country, though my chance is now 220
To use it for my time: I am a brother
Of gracious order, late come from the See
In special business from his Holiness.

Escalus   What news abroad i' th'world?

Duke   None, but that there is so great a fever on good- 225
ness, that the dissolution of it must cure it.

204–5. *come Philip and Jacob:* next 1 May, a popular feast day.
206. *abuse:* ill-use.
207. *of much licence:* who has too much liberty.
212. *furnished with divines:* provided with priests.
212–13. *charitable preparation:* preparation for death in accordance with Christian
    charity.
213. *wrought by my pity:* worked on my principle of compassion.
216. *entertainment:* reception.
220. *chance:* fortune.
222. *the See:* Rome, the Holy See.
223. *his Holiness:* sc. the Pope.
225–33. *None . . . runs the wisdom of the world:* this is a difficult speech since the
    Duke is being intentionally cryptic and may also be being sarcastic. The word
    constant is often emended to 'inconstant'.
226. *that the dissolution of it must cure it:* that only the destruction of goodness can
    cure it from its fever.

Novelty is only in request, and it is as dangerous
to be aged in any kind of course, as it is virtuous
to be constant in any undertaking. There is scarce
truth enough alive to make societies secure; but 230
security enough to make fellowships accurst.
Much upon this riddle runs the wisdom of the
world. This news is old enough, yet it is every
day's news. I pray you, sir, of what disposition
was the Duke?   235

Escalus   One that above all other strifes contended
especially to know himself.

Duke   What pleasure was he give to?

Escalus   Rather rejoicing to see another merry, than merry
at any thing which professed to make him rejoice: 240
a gentleman of all temperance. But leave we him
to his events, with a prayer they may prove
prosperous, and let me desire to know how you
find Claudio prepared. I am made to understand
that you have lent him visitation.   245

Duke   He professes to have received no sinister measure
from his judge, but most willingly humbles himself to the determination of justice; yet had he
framed to himself, by the instruction of his frailty,
many deceiving promises of life, which I, by my 250
good leisure, have discredited to him; and now

---

227. *Novelty:* new fashion.
228. *to be aged in:* to persevere in.
231. *security:* confidence, want of caution.   *fellowships:* societies.
234. *disposition:* temperament.
236. *strifes:* endeavours.   *contended:* strove.
240. *professed:* claimed, attempted.
241. *temperance:* moderation.
242. *his events:* the outcome of his affairs.
246. *professes:* declares, openly acknowledges.
246. *sinister measure:* unfair treatment.
248. *determination:* sentence.
248–9. *yet had he . . . frailty:* but, prompted by human weakness, he had thought
up.
250–1. *which I . . . to him:* which I, by making good use of my spare time, have
shown him to be worthless.

	is he resolved to die.	
Escalus	You have paid the heavens your function, and the	
	prisoner the very debt of your calling. I have	
	laboured for the poor gentleman to the extremest	255
	shore of my modesty, but my brother justice have	
	I found so severe that he hath forced me to tell	
	him he is indeed Justice.	
Duke	If his own life answer the straitness of his proceed-	
	ing, it shall become him well; wherein if he	260
	chance to fail, he hath sentenced himself.	
Escalus	I am going to visit the prisoner. Fare you well.	
Duke	Peace be with you! (*Exeunt Escalus and Provost*	
	He who the sword of heaven will bear	
	Should be as holy as severe;	265
	Pattern in himself to know,	
	Grace to stand, and virtue go:	
	More nor less to others paying	
	Than by self-offences weighing.	
	Shame to him whose cruel striking	270
	Kills for faults of his own liking!	
	Twice treble shame on Angelo,	

253–4. *You have . . . calling:* you have carried out your office in a way which should satisfy both Heaven and Claudio.

255–6. *to the extremest shore of my modesty:* as far as I could presume to go.

258. *he is indeed Justice:* cf. *Introduction*, p. 33.

259. *straitness:* strictness.

264–85. *He who the sword . . . And perform an old contracting:* see *Commentary 15*.

264. *the sword of heaven:* cf. II, ii, 60.

266. *Pattern:* an example or model deserving imitation.

267. *stand:* hold oneself upright.   *go:* act, proceed.

267. *Grace . . . go:* This line has been variously interpreted. It makes good grammatical sense if 'and' is taken to mean 'if' or 'even if', both Shakespearean usages. However, it seems probable that the Duke is distinguishing between 'grace', the condition in which man is strengthened by a divine influence which enables him to withstand temptation, and 'virtue', a more active quality which should shine out and help others (cf. I, i, 34–6). Grammatical correctness would require 'to' before 'go' as in the previous infinitive 'to stand', but grammar is often sacrificed to rhythm in this sort of formal archaic verse.

268–9. *More nor less . . . weighing:* punishing others no more heavily or lightly than he deals with his own offences.

271. *faults of his own liking:* faults in which he took pleasure.

To weed my vice and let his grow!
O, what may man within him hide,
Though angel on the outward side!   275
How may likeness made in crimes,
Making practice on the times,
To draw with idle spiders' strings
Most ponderous and substantial things!
Craft against vice I must apply: 280
With Angelo tonight shall lie
His old betrothed, but despised;
So disguise shall, by the disguised,
Pay with falsehood false exacting,
And perform an old contracting.   (*Exit* 285

273. *my vice:* the Duke may be referring either to the vice which he had neglected
to punish or more generally to the vice of 'everyman'.
276–9. *How may likeness . . . substantial things:* the meaning of these four lines has
never been satisfactorily explained and it may well be that a couplet is
missing. (See *Commentary 2*, 'The Text of *Measure for Measure*'.) It is not even
certain whether the lines refer back to the Duke's reflection on Angelo, or
forward to his resolve to trap him.
277. *practice:* trickery.
283–5. *So disguise . . . an old contracting:* so Mariana in disguise will use deceit to
falsely pay Angelo's illegal demand and in so doing will fulfil an old contract.

ACT IV

SCENE I. *The Moated Grange*

Enter MARIANA *and a* BOY

BOY *sings*

Take, oh take those lips away,
    That so sweetly were forsworn;
And those eyes, the break of day,
    Lights that do mislead the morn:
But my kisses bring again, bring again;   5
Seals of love, but seal'd in vain, seal'd in vain.

Mariana   Break off thy song, and haste thee quick away,
Here comes a man of comfort, whose advice
Hath often still'd my brawling discontent.
                                   (Exit Boy

Enter DUKE *disguised as before*

    I cry you mercy, sir, and well could wish   10
You had not found me here so musical:
Let me excuse me, and believe me so,
My mirth it much displeased, but pleased my woe.

Duke   'Tis good; though music oft hath such a charm
To make bad good, and good provoke to harm.   15
I pray you tell me, hath any body enquired for
me here today? Much upon this time have I
promised here to meet.

Mariana   You have not been enquired after: I have sat here
all day.   20

---

2. *forsworn:* perjured.
9. *still'd:* subdued.   *brawling:* discordant.
10. *cry you mercy:* beg your pardon.
14–15. *music oft . . . provoke to harm:* music often has a magic which can make bad
    seem good and can lead virtue astray.

Enter ISABELLA

Duke	I do constantly believe you: the time is come even now. I shall crave your forbearance a little: may be I will call upon you anon for some advantage to yourself.
Mariana	I am always bound to you. (*Exit* 25
Duke	Very well met, and well come. What is the news from this good Deputy?
Isabella	He hath a garden circummured with brick, Whose western side is with a vineyard back'd; And to that vineyard is a planched gate, 30 That makes his opening with this bigger key. This other doth command a little door Which from the vineyard to the garden leads; There have I made my promise Upon the heavy middle of the night 35 To call upon him.
Duke	But shall you on your knowledge find this way?
Isabella	I have ta'en a due and wary note upon 't; With whispering and most guilty diligence, In action all of precept, he did show me 40 The way twice o'er.
Duke	Are there no other tokens Between you 'greed concerning her observance?
Isabella	No, none; but only a repair i' th' dark,

21. *constantly:* confidently.
22. *crave your forbearance a little:* ask you to withdraw for a short time.
23. *anon:* soon.
25. *I am always bound to you:* I am ever under obligation to you.
28. *circummured:* walled round.
30. *planched:* boarded.
31. *That makes his opening:* that is opened.
32. *doth command:* controls.
38. *due:* proper.   *wary:* careful.
39. *diligence:* thoroughness.
40. *In action all of precept:* with gestures amounting to a written description.
41. *tokens:* signals.
42. *'greed:* agreed.   *her observance:* what she must do.
43. *repair:* journey.

And that I have possess'd him my most stay
Can be but brief: for I have made him know   45
I have a servant comes with me along
That stays upon me, whose persuasion is
I come about my brother.

Duke   'Tis well borne up.
I have not yet made known to Mariana
A word of this. What ho, within! Come forth!   50

Re-enter MARIANA

I pray you, be acquainted with this maid;
She comes to do you good.

Isabella   I do desire the like.
Duke   Do you persuade yourself that I respect you?
Mariana   Good friar, I know you do, and have found it.
Duke   Take, then, this your companion by the hand,   55
Who hath a story ready for your ear.
I shall attend your leisure, but make haste;
The vaporous night approaches.
Mariana   Will't please you walk aside?

(Exeunt Mariana and Isabella

Duke   O place and greatness! Millions of false eyes   60
Are stuck upon thee; volumes of report
Run with these false and most contrarious quests
Upon thy doings: thousand escapes of wit
Make thee the father of their idle dream
And rack thee in their fancies.

44. *possess'd:* informed. *most:* longest.
47. *stays upon:* waits for. *whose persuasion is:* who believes.
48. *borne up:* carried out.
53. *Do you persuade yourself:* do you believe.
60–5. *O place and greatness . . . their fancies:* see Commentary 16.
60–1. *Millions . . . upon thee:* you are being watched by a great number of dis-
     honest subjects.
61–3. *volumes of report . . . Upon thy doings:* lengthy rumours result from these
     untrue and pernicious enquiries into your life.
63–5. *thousand escapes . . . in their fancies:* many clever stories are dreamed up
     about you, the dreamers distorting your image in their fantasies.

Re-enter MARIANA *and* ISABELLA

	Welcome, how agreed?	65

Isabella   She'll take the enterprise upon her, father,
If you advise it.

Duke   It is not my consent,
But my entreaty too.

Isabella   Little have you to say
When you depart from him, but, soft and low,
'Remember now my brother'.

Mariana   Fear me not.   70

Duke   Nor, gentle daughter, fear you not at all.
He is your husband on a pre-contract:
To bring you thus together, 'tis no sin,
Sith that the justice of your title to him
Doth flourish the deceit. Come, let us go;   75
Our corn's to reap, for yet our tithe's to sow.

                           (*Exeunt*

SCENE II. *A Room in the Prison*

Enter PROVOST *and* POMPEY

Provost   Come hither, sirrah. Can you cut off a man's
head?

Pompey   If the man be a bachelor, sir, I can; but if he be a
married man, he's his wife's head, and I can never
cut off a woman's head.   5

Provost   Come, sir, leave me your snatches, and yield me
a direct answer. Tomorrow morning are to die
Claudio and Barnardine. Here is in our prison a
common executioner, who in his office lacks a

---

72. *a pre-contract:* see *Commentary 10*, 'Elizabethan Marriage Contracts'.
74–5. *Sith . . . deceit:* since the deceitfulness of the act is vindicated by the justice
    of your claim to be Angelo's wife.
76. *Our corn's . . . to sow:* we must labour before we can reap a reward.

6. *snatches:* witticisms.

	helper. If you will take it on you to assist him, it 10 shall redeem you from your gyves; if not, you shall have your full time of imprisonment, and your deliverance with an unpitied whipping; for you have been a notorious bawd.
Pompey	Sir, I have been an unlawful bawd time out of 15 mind, but yet I will be content to be a lawful hangman. I would be glad to receive some instruction from my fellow partner.
Provost	What, ho, Abhorson! Where's Abhorson, there?

Enter ABHORSON

Abhorson	Do you call, sir? 20
Provost	Sirrah, here's a fellow will help you tomorrow in your execution. If you think it meet, compound with him by the year, and let him abide here with you; if not, use him for the present, and dismiss him. He cannot plead his estimation 25 with you: he hath been a bawd.
Abhorson	A bawd, sir? Fie upon him, he will discredit our mystery.
Provost	Go to, sir; you weigh equally; a feather will turn the scale. (*Exit* 30
Pompey	Pray, sir, by your good favour—for surely, sir, a good favour you have, but that you have a hanging look—do you call, sir, your occupation a mystery?
Abhorson	Ay, sir, a mystery. 35

11. *gyves:* shackles.
13. *deliverance:* release. *unpitied:* unmerciful.
22. *meet:* fitting.
22–3. *compound with him by the year:* make a year's contract with him.
25–6. *He cannot plead his estimation with you:* he cannot argue that his social status is superior to yours.
27–8. *he will discredit our mystery:* he will bring the profession of hangman into disrepute.
28. *mystery:* skill or profession.
29. *you weigh equally:* your professions are both equally disreputable.
32. *favour:* face, countenance. *but:* except.

Pompey	Painting, sir, I have heard say, is a mystery; and your whores, sir, being members of my occupation, using painting, do prove my occupation a mystery: but what mystery there should be in hanging, if I should be hanged, I cannot imagine. 40
Abhorson	Sir, it is a mystery.
Pompey	Proof?
Abhorson	Every true man's apparel fits your thief. If it be too little for your thief, your true man thinks it big enough. If it be too big for your thief, your 45 thief thinks it little enough. So every true man's apparel fits your thief.

Re-enter PROVOST

Provost	Are you agreed?
Pompey	Sir, I will serve him; for I do find your hangman is a more penitent trade than your bawd: he doth 50 oftener ask forgiveness.
Provost	You, sirrah, provide your block and your axe tomorrow four o'clock.
Abhorson	Come on, bawd, I will instruct thee in my trade. Follow. 55
Pompey	I do desire to learn, sir: and I hope, if you have occasion to use me for your own turn, you shall find me yare. For truly, sir, for your kindness I

36–41. *Painting . . . a mystery:* Pompey proves that prostitution is a mystery by a simple misuse of logic: painting is a skilled craft; prostitutes paint; therefore their trade is a skilled one.

38. *using painting:* i.e. applying cosmetics.

43–7. *Every true man . . . thief:* Abhorson attempts to prove that hanging is also a mystery. His 'logic' is impossible to follow and it may well be that a crucial part of his argument is missing (see *Commentary 2*, 'The Text of *Measure for Measure*'). His 'proof' seems to centre on the fact that hangmen had a right to the clothing of the prisoners whom they executed.

51. *ask forgiveness:* it was the custom for the hangman to ask for the forgiveness of the condemned man before executing him.

52. *provide:* have ready.

56–7. *if you . . . for your own turn:* i.e. should I be asked to execute you.

58. *yare:* ready.

	owe you a good turn.	
Provost	Call hither Barnardine and Claudio.	60

(Exeunt Pompey and Abhorson

The one has my pity; not a jot the other—
Being a murderer—though he were my brother.

Enter CLAUDIO

Look, here's the warrant, Claudio, for thy death;
'Tis now dead midnight, and by eight tomorrow
Thou must be made immortal. Where's Barnar-
    dine?   65

Claudio   As fast lock'd up in sleep as guiltless labour
When it lies starkly in the traveller's bones.
He will not wake.

Provost   Who can do good on him?
Well, go, prepare yourself. (*Knocking within*) But,
    hark, what noise?
Heaven give your spirits comfort! (*Exit Claudio*)
    By and by.   70
I hope it is some pardon or reprieve
For the most gentle Claudio.

Enter DUKE disguised as before

                   Welcome, father.

Duke   The best and wholesomest spirits of the night
Envelop you, good Provost! Who call'd here of
    late?

Provost   None since the curfew rung.   75

Duke   Not Isabel?

Provost   No.

Duke   They will then, ere't be long.

Provost   What comfort is for Claudio?

Duke   There's some in hope.

67. *starkly:* stiffly.

Provost	It is a bitter deputy.
Duke	Not so, not so; his life is parallel'd 80
	Even with the stroke and line of his great justice.
	He doth with holy abstinence subdue
	That in himself which he spurs on his power
	To qualify in others: were he meal'd with that
	Which he corrects, then were he tyrannous; 85
	But this being so, he's just. (*Knocking within*
	Now are they come.
	(*Exit Provost*
	This is a gentle provost; seldom when
	The steelèd gaoler is the friend of men.
	(*Knocking within*
	How now! What noise? That spirit's possess'd
	with haste
	That wounds the unsisting postern with these
	strokes. 90

Re-enter PROVOST

Provost	There he must stay until the officer
	Arise to let him in: he is call'd up.
Duke	Have you no countermand for Claudio yet,
	But he must die tomorrow?
Provost	None sir, none.
Duke	As near the dawning, provost, as it is, 95
	You shall hear more ere morning.
Provost	Happily
	You something know; yet I believe there comes

79. *bitter:* harsh.
80–1. *his life . . . his great justice:* Angelo's private life is as virtuous as the justice
     which he administers. The Duke's comment is, of course, ironic.
84. *qualify:* moderate.   *meal'd:* spotted.
88. *steelèd:* hardened.
90. *That . . . strokes:* that knocks upon the door.   *unsisting:* unresisting.   *postern:*
     small side or back door.
91. *he:* i.e. the messenger.
93. *countermand:* command revoking the order to execute Claudio.
96. *Happily:* haply, i.e. perhaps.

No countermand; no such example have we.
Besides, upon the very siege of justice
Lord Angelo hath to the public ear   100
Profess'd the contrary.

Enter a MESSENGER

This is his lordship's man.

Duke	And here comes Claudio's pardon.
Messenger	My lord hath sent you this note, and by me this further charge: that you swerve not from the smallest article of it, neither in time, matter, or 105 other circumstance. Good morrow; for, as I take it, it is almost day.
Provost	I shall obey him. (*Exit Messenger*
Duke	(*Aside*) This is his pardon, purchased by such sin For which the pardoner himself is in. 110 Hence hath offence his quick celerity, When it is borne in high authority. When vice makes mercy, mercy's so extended, That for the fault's love is th'offender friended. Now, sir, what news? 115
Provost	I told you: Lord Angelo, belike thinking me remiss in mine office, awakens me with this unwonted putting-on; methinks strangely, for he hath not used it before.
Duke	Pray you, let's hear. 120
Provost	(*Reads*)

Whatsoever you may hear to the contrary, let

99. *siege:* seat.
109–10. *This . . . himself is in:* this is Claudio's pardon obtained by Angelo (the pardoner) committing the same sin which led to Claudio's conviction.
111–12. *Hence . . . high authority:* offence is easily committed by someone in a position of authority.
113–14. *When vice . . . friended:* the kind of mercy which is born of vice is a distorted mercy which forgives the offender through love of the fault.   *extended:* strained.
116. *belike:* probably.
116–17. *remiss:* negligent.
117–18. *unwonted putting on:* unaccustomed exhortation.

Claudio be executed by four of the clock, and in
the afternoon Barnardine. For my better satisfaction, let me have Claudio's head sent me by
five. Let this be duly performed, with a thought 125
that more depends on it than we must yet deliver.
Thus fail not to do your office, as you will answer
it at your peril.
What say you to this, sir?

Duke   What is that Barnardine who is to be executed in 130
the afternoon?

Provost   A Bohemian born, but here nursed up and bred;
one that is a prisoner nine years old.

Duke   How came it that the absent Duke had not either
delivered him to his liberty or executed him? I 135
have heard it was ever his manner to do so.

Provost   His friends still wrought reprieves for him; and
indeed, his fact till now in the government of
Lord Angelo came not to an undoubtful proof.

Duke   It is now apparent?   140

Provost   Most manifest, and not denied by himself.

Duke   Hath he borne himself penitently in prison? How
seems he to be touched?

Provost   A man that apprehends death no more dreadfully
but as a drunken sleep; careless, reckless, and 145
fearless of what's past, present, or to come;
insensible of mortality, and desperately mortal.

126. *deliver:* announce, tell.
133. *is a prisoner nine years old:* has been in prison for nine years.
137. *wrought:* obtained.
138–9. *his fact . . . an undoubtful proof:* his crime was not proved beyond doubt
     until now, under the rule of Angelo.
138. *fact:* deed.
140. *apparent:* plain, evident.
141. *manifest:* clear, obvious.
143. *touched:* affected.
144. *apprehends:* imagines, thinks of.
147. *insensible . . . mortal:* quite insensitive to the idea of death yet about to die
     in a desperate state.
147. *desperately:* without hope.

Duke	He wants advice.
Provost	He will hear none. He hath evermore had the liberty of the prison; give him leave to escape 150 hence, he would not. Drunk many times a day, if not many days entirely drunk. We have very oft awaked him, as if to carry him to execution, and showed him a seeming warrant for it; it hath not moved him at all. 155
Duke	More of him anon. There is written in your brow, provost, honesty and constancy; if I read it not truly, my ancient skill beguiles me. But in the boldness of my cunning, I will lay my self in hazard. Claudio, whom here you have warrant to 160 execute, is no greater forfeit to the law than Angelo who hath sentenced him. To make you understand this in a manifested effect, I crave but four days' respite: for the which you are to do me both a present and a dangerous courtesy. 165
Provost	Pray sir, in what?
Duke	In the delaying death.
Provost.	Alack, how may I do it? Having the hour limited, and an express command, under penalty, to deliver his head in the view of Angelo? I may 170 make my case as Claudio's, to cross this in the smallest.

148. *He wants advice:* he needs spiritual guidance.
149. *evermore:* always.
150–1. *give . . . he would not:* if you gave him an opportunity to escape from the prison he would not want it.
154. *seeming:* apparent.
158. *beguiles:* deceives.
158–60. *in the boldness . . . myself in hazard:* confident in my ability to read character I will take a personal risk.
159. *cunning:* knowledge, skill.
161. *is no greater forfeit to the law:* is not more guilty in the eyes of the law.
163. *in a manifested effect:* as a proved fact.
164. *respite:* delay.
165. *present:* immediate. *courtesy:* service.
169. *limited:* appointed. *express:* exact.
170–2. *I may make . . . in the smallest:* i.e. I too shall probably be sentenced to death if I disobey instructions in any way.

Duke	By the vow of mine order I warrant you, if my instructions may be your guide. Let this Barnardine be this morning executed, and his head borne 175 to Angelo.
Provost	Angelo hath seen them both, and will discover the favour.
Duke	O, death's a great disguiser; and you may add to it. Shave the head, and tie the beard, and say it 180 was the desire of the penitent to be so bared before his death: you know the course is common. If any thing fall to you upon this, more than thanks and good fortune, by the Saint whom I profess, I will plead against it with my life. 185
Provost	Pardon me, good father; it is against my oath.
Duke	Were you sworn to the Duke, or to the Deputy?
Provost	To him, and to his substitutes.
Duke	You will think you have made no offence if the Duke avouch the justice of your dealing? 190
Provost	But what likelihood is in that?
Duke	Not a resemblance, but a certainty. Yet, since I see you fearful, that neither my coat, integrity, nor persuasion can with ease attempt you, I will go further than I meant, to pluck all fears out of 195 you. Look you, sir, here is the hand and seal of the Duke: you know the character, I doubt not,

173. *I warrant you:* I give you security.
177. *discover:* discern, distinguish.
178. *favour:* face.
181. *bared:* shaved.
182. *the course is common:* it is a common custom.
183. *fall:* happen.
184. *by the Saint whom I profess:* by the patron saint of my order.
185. *I will plead against it with my life:* I will be prepared to sacrifice my life in your defence.
190. *avouch:* assure, guarantee.
192. *resemblance:* likelihood.
193. *coat:* friar's habit.
194. *attempt:* move.
196. *hand:* handwriting.
197. *character:* writing.

	and the signet is not strange to you.
Provost	I know them both.
Duke	The contents of this is the return of the Duke: 200

you shall anon over-read it at your pleasure;
where you shall find within these two days he will
be here. This is a thing that Angelo knows not;
for he this very day receives letters of strange
tenour, perchance of the Duke's death, perchance 205
entering into some monastery; but, by chance,
nothing of what is writ. Look, the unfolding star
calls up the shepherd. Put not yourself into
amazement how these things should be: all
difficulties are but easy when they are known. 210
Call your executioner, and off with Barnardine's
head. I will give him a present shrift and advise
him for a better place. Yet you are amazed; but
this shall absolutely resolve you. Come away; it
is almost clear dawn.   (*Exeunt* 215

SCENE III. *Another Room in the Prison*

Enter POMPEY

Pompey	I am as well acquainted here as I was in our house

of profession: one would think it were Mistress
Overdone's own house, for here be many of her
old customers. First, here's young Master Rash;

205. *tenour:* drift of meaning.
205. *perchance:* perhaps.
206–7. *but . . . what is writ:* but, as it happens, nothing of the truth (as is written in this other letter).
207–8. *Look . . . the shepherd:* the morning star tells the shepherd that it is time to release his sheep from their fold.
212. *a present shrift:* an immediate confession and absolution.
212–13. *advise him for a better place:* prepare him for heaven.
214. *absolutely resolve you:* completely dispel your doubts.

1–20. See *Commentary 17* for the significance of the Proper names.
1–2. *I am . . . house of profession:* I know as many people here as I did in the brothel.

he's in for a commodity of brown paper and old 5
ginger, nine-score and seventeen pounds; of which
he made five marks, ready money: marry, then
ginger was not much in request, for the old women
were all dead. Then is there here one Master
Caper, at the suit of Master Three-pile the mercer, 10
for some four suits of peach-coloured satin, which
now peaches him a beggar. Then have we here
young Dizy, and young Master Deep-vow, and
Master Copper-spur, and Master Starve-lackey
the rapier and dagger man, and young Drop-heir 15
that killed lusty Pudding, and Master Forthright
the tilter, and brave Master Shoe-tie the great
traveller, and wild Half-can that stabbed Pots, and,
I think, forty more, all great doers in our trade,
and are now 'for the Lord's sake'. 20

Enter ABHORSON

Abhorson	Sirrah, bring Barnardine hither.
Pompey	Master Barnardine! You must rise and be hanged, Master Barnardine!
Abhorson	What ho, Barnardine!
Barnardine	(*Within*) A pox o' your throats! Who makes that 25 noise there? What are you?
Pompey	Your friends, sir; the hangman. You must be so good, sir, to rise and be put to death.

5-9. *he's in . . . were all dead:* to evade government restrictions on money-lending, usurers sometimes lent merchandise instead of money. Master Rash, at the mercy of a usurer, found himself burdened with £197 worth of brown paper and old ginger which, since there was no demand for paper and ginger, sold for only £3.33 (the mark being valued at 67p).

5. *commodity:* consignment.

8-9. *ginger . . . were all dead:* presumably a now obscure allusion to some particular use which old women had for ginger.

10. *mercer:* cloth merchant.

12. *peaches him a beggar:* denounces him as a beggar.

19. *all great doers in our trade:* all regular customers at the brothel.

20. *'for the Lord's sake':* this was the prisoners' cry for alms.

25. *A pox o' your throats:* curse you for shouting.

Barnardine	(*Within*) Away, you rogue, away, I am sleepy.
Abhorson	Tell him he must awake, and that quickly too. 30
Pompey	Pray, Master Barnardine, awake till you are executed, and sleep afterwards.
Abhorson	Go in to him, and fetch him out.
Pompey	He is coming, sir, he is coming: I hear his straw rustle. 35
Abhorson	Is the axe upon the block, sirrah?
Pompey	Very ready, sir.

Enter BARNADINE

Barnardine	How now, Abhorson? What's the news with you?
Abhorson	Truly, sir, I would desire you to clap into your 40 prayers: for look you, the warrant's come.
Barnardine	You rogue, I have been drinking all night; I am not fitted for't.
Pompey	O, the better, sir: for he that drinks all night and is hanged betimes in the morning may sleep the 45 sounder all the next day.
Abhorson	Look you, sir, here comes your ghostly father: do we jest now, think you?

Enter DUKE *disguised as before*

Duke	Sir, induced by my charity, and hearing how hastily you are to depart, I am come to advise you, 50 comfort you, and pray with you.
Barnardine	Friar, not I: I have been drinking hard all night, and I will have more time to prepare me, or they shall beat out my brains with billets. I will not consent to die this day, that's certain. 55
Duke	O, sir, you must: and therefore I beseech you

40–1. *clap into your prayers*: briskly start praying.
45. *betimes*: early.
47. *ghostly*: spiritual.
54. *billets*: heavy sticks.

	Look forward on the journey you shall go.	
Barnardine	I swear I will not die today for any man's persua-	
	sion.	
Duke	But hear you—	60
Barnardine	Not a word: if you have any thing to say to me,	
	come to my ward; for thence will not I today.	

(Exit

Duke	Unfit to live or die: O gravel heart!
	After him, fellows, bring him to the block.

(Exeunt Abhorson and Pompey

Enter PROVOST

Provost	Now sir, how do you find the prisoner?	65
Duke	A creature unprepared, unmeet for death;	
	And to transport him in the mind he is	
	Were damnable.	
Provost	Here in the prison, father,	
	There died this morning of a cruel fever	
	One Ragozine, a most notorious pirate,	70
	A man of Claudio's years; his beard and head	
	Just of his colour. What if we do omit	
	This reprobate till he were well inclined,	
	And satisfy the deputy with the visage	
	Of Ragozine, more like to Claudio?	75
Duke	O, 'tis an accident that heaven provides.	
	Dispatch it presently; the hour draws on	
	Prefix'd by Angelo. See this be done,	
	And sent according to command, whiles I	
	Persuade this rude wretch willingly to die.	80

62. *ward:* cell.
63. *gravel:* stony, hard.
66. *unmeet:* unfit.
67. *to transport him:* to move him from this world to the next.
72. *omit:* ignore.
73. *well inclined:* ready to die.
76. *accident:* event.
77. *Dispatch it presently:* carry it out at once.
78. *Prefix'd:* fixed in advance.

Provost	This shall be done, good father, presently.
	But Barnardine must die this afternoon;
	And how shall we continue Claudio,
	To save me from the danger that might come
	If he were known alive?
Duke	Let this be done. 85
	Put them in secret holds, both Barnardine and
	Claudio.
	Ere twice the sun hath made his journal greeting
	To the under generation, you shall find
	Your safety manifested.
Provost	I am your free dependant. 90
Duke	Quick, dispatch, and send the head to Angelo.

(*Exit Provost*

Now will I write letters to Angelo—
The provost, he shall bear them—whose contents
Shall witness to him I am near at home,
And that, by great injunctions, I am bound   95
To enter publicly. Him I'll desire
To meet me at the consecrated fount,
A league below the city; and from thence,
By cold gradation and well-balanced form,
We shall proceed with Angelo.   100

Re-enter PROVOST

Provost	Here is the head; I'll carry it myself.
Duke	Convenient is it. Make a swift return;

81. *presently:* immediately.
83. *continue:* keep.
86. *holds:* cells.
87–8. *Ere twice . . . under generation:* before two days have passed.
87. *journal:* daily.
88. *under generation:* the race who live on the lower side of the world.
90. *free dependant:* willing assistant.
94. *witness to him:* show to Angelo.
95. *injunctions:* laws.
99–100. *By cold gradation . . . with Angelo:* 'proceed' refers not only to the pro-
cession but also to the process by which Angelo will be tried in Act V. *cold
gradation:* steady, formal progress. *well-balanced form:* unbiased procedure.
102. *Convenient:* fitting.

	For I would commune with you of such things	
	That want no ear but yours.	
Provost	I'll make all speed.	
	(*Exit*	
Isabella	(*Within*) Peace, ho, be here!	105
Duke	The tongue of Isabel. She's come to know	
	If yet her brother's pardon be come hither;	
	But I will keep her ignorant of her good,	
	To make her heavenly comforts of despair,	
	When it is least expected.	

Enter ISABELLA

Isabella	Ho, by your leave!	110
Duke	Good morning to you, fair and gracious daughter.	
Isabella	The better, given me by so holy a man.	
	Hath yet the Deputy sent my brother's pardon?	
Duke	He hath released him, Isabel, from the world;	
	His head is off, and sent to Angelo.	115
Isabella	Nay, but it is not so.	
Duke	It is no other. Show your wisdom, daughter,	
	In your close patience.	
Isabella	O, I will to him and pluck out his eyes!	
Duke	You shall not be admitted to his sight.	120
Isabella	Unhappy Claudio! wretched Isabel!	
	Injurious world! most damnèd Angelo!	
Duke	This nor hurts him nor profits you a jot;	
	Forbear it therefore; give your cause to heaven.	
	Mark what I say, which you shall find	125
	By every syllable a faithful verity.	
	The Duke comes home tomorrow; nay, dry your	
	eyes;	

103. *commune:* talk over.
104. *That want no ear but yours:* that only you must hear.
109. *of despair:* out of despair.
118. *close:* uncommunicative.
124. *Forbear:* stop. *give your cause to heaven:* leave it to God to punish Angelo.
126. *By every syllable a faithful verity:* absolutely true.

One of our covent, and his confessor,
Gives me this instance: already he hath carried
Notice to Escalus and Angelo,   130
Who do prepare to meet him at the gates,
There to give up their power. If you can, pace
    your wisdom
In that good path that I would wish it go,
And you shall have your bosom on this wretch,
Grace of the Duke, revenges to your heart,   135
And general honour.

Isabella   I am directed by you.
Duke   This letter then to Friar Peter give;
'Tis that he sent me of the Duke's return:
Say, by this token, I desire his company
At Mariana's house tonight. Her cause and yours 140
I'll perfect him withal, and he shall bring you
Before the Duke; and to the head of Angelo
Accuse him home and home. For my poor self,
I am combinèd by a sacred vow,
And shall be absent. Wend you with this letter: 145
Command these fretting waters from your eyes
With a light heart; trust not my holy order,
If I pervert your course—Who's here?

Enter LUCIO

Lucio   Good even. Friar, where's the provost?
Duke   Not within, sir.   150
Lucio   O pretty Isabella, I am pale at mine heart to see

128. *covent:* i.e. convent; cf. Covent Garden.
129. *instance:* proof.
132–3. *pace your wisdom . . . wish it go:* wisely follow the good course of action
    which I advise.
134. *your bosom:* i.e. all the satisfaction you desire.
141. *I'll perfect him withal:* I'll give him complete information about.
142–3. *and to . . . home and home:* and to his face accuse him plainly and directly.
144. *combinèd:* bound.
145. *Wend:* go.
146. *Command . . . eyes:* Stop your tears. *fretting:* wearing away.
148. *pervert:* misdirect.
151. *pale at mine heart:* terrified, frightened.

thine eyes so red: thou must be patient. I am fain
to dine and sup with water and bran: I dare not
for my head fill my belly: one fruitful meal
would set me to't. But they say the Duke will 155
be here tomorrow. By my troth, Isabel, I loved
thy brother; if the old fantastical Duke of dark
corners had been at home, he had lived.

(Exit Isabella

Duke	Sir, the Duke is marvellous little beholding to your reports; but the best is, he lives not in them. 160
Lucio	Friar, thou knowest not the Duke so well as I do; he's a better woodman than thou takest him for.
Duke	Well, you'll answer this one day. Fare ye well.
Lucio	Nay, tarry, I'll go along with thee: I can tell 165 thee pretty tales of the Duke.
Duke	You have told me too many of him already, sir, if they be true; if not true, none were enough.
Lucio	I was once before him for getting a wench with child. 170
Duke	Did you such a thing?
Lucio	Yes, marry, did I; but I was fain to forswear it; they would else have married me to the rotten medlar.

152–5. *I am fain . . . set me to't:* It was thought that meat aroused the sexual appetite. Lucio says that if he were to have one good meal he would be unable to
control his desire and would be sentenced like Claudio.
152. *fain:* obliged.
157. *fantastical:* fanciful, capricious.
157–8. *of dark corners:* suggesting that the Duke habitually made secret assignations
with women, cf. *Commentary 11*. The phrase is dramatically ironic in that in
his disguise the Duke has indeed been a 'fantastical Duke of dark corners'.
159. *marvellous little beholding:* very little indebted.
160. *he lives not in them:* he does not lead the kind of life which you have attributed
to him.
162. *woodman:* woman hunter.
169. *before him:* i.e. for judgment.
172. *marry:* indeed, to be sure. *fain to forswear:* obliged to deny.
173–4. *the rotten medlar:* the medlar is a fruit which is best eaten overripe; prostitutes were often diseased, hence the analogy.

Duke	Sir, your company is fairer than honest. Rest 175 you well.
Lucio	By my troth, I'll go with thee to the lane's end: if bawdy talk offend you, we'll have very little of it. Nay, friar, I am a kind of burr; I shall stick.

(*Exeunt*

SCENE IV. *A Room in* ANGELO'S *House*

Enter ANGELO *and* ESCALUS

Escalus	Every letter he hath writ hath disvouched other.
Angelo	In most uneven and distracted manner. His actions show much like to madness; pray heaven his wisdom be not tainted. And why meet him at the gates and redeliver our authorities there? 5
Escalus	I guess not.
Angelo	And why should we proclaim it in an hour before his entering, that if any crave redress of injustice, they should exhibit their petitions in the street?
Escalus	He shows his reason for that: to have a dispatch 10 of complaints, and to deliver us from devices hereafter, which shall then have no power to stand against us.
Angelo	Well, I beseech you, let it be proclaimed betimes i' th'morn; I'll call you at your house: give notice 15 to such men of sort and suit as are to meet him.

175. *fairer:* a reminder that Lucio is 'a fantastic' and hence dressed very ostentatiously.

1. *disvouched:* contradicted.
2. *uneven:* confused, disordered.   *distracted:* crazy, mad.
4. *tainted:* impaired.
5. *redeliver:* hand back.
8. *crave:* beg.   *redress:* reparation.
9. *exhibit:* submit.
10. *dispatch:* immediate settlement.
11–13. *to deliver us . . . against us:* to protect us by dealing with any false charges which might otherwise be brought against us later.
16. *men of sort and suit:* men of position and with a retinue.

Escalus	I shall, sir. Fare you well.
Angelo	Good night. (*Exit Escalus*

This deed unshapes me quite, makes me un-
    pregnant
And dull to all proceedings. A deflower'd maid,   20
And by an eminent body that enforced
The law against it! But that her tender shame
Will not proclaim against her maiden loss,
How might she tongue me! Yet reason dares her
    no;
For my authority bears of a credent bulk,   25
That no particular scandal once can touch
But it confounds the breather. He should have
    lived,
Save that his riotous youth, with dangerous sense,
Might in the times to come have ta'en revenge
By so receiving a dishonour'd life   30
With ransom of such shame. Would yet he had
    lived!
Alack, when once our grace we have forgot,
Nothing goes right; we would, and we would not.
                           (*Exit*

---

19. *This deed:* Angelo is referring to his supposed seduction of Isabella. *unshapes me quite:* has completely shattered me. *unpregnant:* unready.
20. *dull:* insensitive. *proceedings:* business. *deflower'd:* violated, seduced.
21. *an eminent body:* a person of high rank.
22. *it:* i.e. sexual offence.
22–4. *But that . . . tongue me:* were it not that her youthful modesty will prevent her from publicly announcing her lost virginity, how she might cry out against me.
24. *reason dares her no:* reason will prevent her.
25–7. *For . . . confounds the breather:* my authority constitutes an outward covering whereby anything I say will be believed so that any personal attack made upon me will result in the destruction of the person who utters it.
25. *credent:* credible. *bulk:* a technical term for the framework projecting from the front of a shop.
26. *particular:* private, personal.
27. *He:* Claudio.
28. *Save:* except, but. *sense:* passion, feeling.
32. *grace:* sense of duty, integrity.
33. *we would, and we would not:* we do not know what we want.

SCENE V. *Outside the City*

Enter DUKE, *no longer in disguise, and* FRIAR PETER

Duke	These letters at fit time deliver me. (*Giving letters*
	The provost knows our purpose and our plot;
	The matter being afoot, keep your instruction,
	And hold you ever to our special drift,
	Though sometimes you do blench from this to that, 5
	As cause doth minister. Go call at Flavius' house,
	And tell him where I stay: give the like notice
	To Valentius, Rowland, and to Crassus,
	And bid them bring the trumpets to the gate;
	But send me Flavius first.
Friar Peter	It shall be speeded well. 10
	(*Exit*

Enter VARRIUS

Duke	I thank thee, Varrius; thou hast made good haste.
	Come, we will walk. There's other of our friends
	Will greet us here anon, my gentle Varrius.
	(*Exeunt*

SCENE VI. *Near the City Gates*

Enter ISABELLA *and* MARIANA

Isabella	To speak so indirectly I am loath;

1. *fit:* appropriate, proper. *deliver me:* deliver for me.
3–4. *The matter . . . special drift:* once the business has started, do as you have been instructed, and always follow our plan.
5–6. *Though . . . minister:* though occasionally altering minor details where necessary.
5. *blench:* start aside, shy.
9. *trumpets:* the Duke's return, unlike his departure, will be announced with pomp and circumstance.
10. *speeded well:* done at once.

1. *To speak . . . loath:* I am unwilling to speak so evasively.

I would say the truth; but to accuse him so,
That is your part; yet I am advised to do it,
He says, to veil full purpose.

Mariana   Be ruled by him.

Isabella   Besides, he tells me that, if peradventure   5
He speak against me on the adverse side,
I should not think it strange; for 'tis a physic
That's bitter to sweet end.

Mariana   I would Friar Peter—

Isabella   O, peace! the friar is come.

Enter FRIAR PETER

Friar Peter   Come, I have found you out a stand most fit,   10
Where you may have such vantage on the Duke
He shall not pass you. Twice have the trumpets
    sounded;
The generous and gravest citizens
Have hent the gates, and very near upon
The Duke is entering: therefore hence, away!   15

                                        (*Exeunt*

2–3. *but . . . your part:* Isabella says that Mariana should denounce Angelo since
    she kept the assignation.
4. *He:* i.e. the Duke.   *to veil full purpose:* to conceal what he really intends to do.
6. *against me on the adverse side:* i.e. in Angelo's defence.
7–8. *for 'tis . . . to sweet end:* it is like a medicine that is unpleasant, but for a good
    purpose.
10. *a stand most fit:* a very convenient position.
11–12. *Where you . . . pass you:* where you will be so well placed that the Duke
    will be unable to pass you by.
13. *generous:* noble.
14. *hent:* occupied, i.e. taken their places at.   *near upon:* soon.

ACT V

Scene I. *The City Gates*

Enter from one side the Duke, Varrius *and other* Lords; *from the other side* Angelo, Escalus, Lucio, *the* Provost, Officers *and* Citizens

Duke	My very worthy cousin, fairly met.
	Our old and faithful friend, we are glad to see you.
Angelo and Escalus	Happy return be to your royal Grace!
Duke	Many and hearty thankings to you both.
	We have made enquiry of you, and we hear 5
	Such goodness of your justice, that our soul
	Cannot but yield you forth to public thanks,
	Forerunning more requital.
Angelo	You make my bonds still greater.
Duke	O, your desert speaks loud, and I should wrong it,
	To lock it in the wards of covert bosom, 10
	When it deserves with characters of brass
	A forted residence 'gainst the tooth of time
	And razure of oblivion. Give me your hand,
	And let the subject see, to make them know

1. *cousin:* a form of address used by sovereigns when addressing noblemen.
4. *thankings:* thanks.
6. *soul:* cf. I, i, 17.
7–8. *Cannot . . . requital:* cannot but reward you by thanking you in public before giving you further payment.
8. *bonds:* obligations; but ironic in that it may also mean 'fetters'.
9. *desert:* deserving.
10. *To lock . . . covert bosom:* to imprison it in the cells of my secret affection. The irony is continued in the prison metaphor.
11–13. *When it . . . And razure of oblivion:* when it should be written up in letters of brass to give it protection against the destructive forces of time and oblivion; cf. Sonnet 64.
12. *forted:* strongly defended.
13. *razure:* obliteration, effacement.
14. *the subject:* the people.

	That outward courtesies would fain proclaim	15
	Favours that keep within. Come, Escalus,	
	You must walk by us on our other hand;	
	And good supporters are you.	

Enter FRIAR PETER, ISABELLA, *behind them* MARIANA, *veiled*

Friar Peter   Now is your time: speak loud, and kneel before
        him.

Isabella   Justice, O royal Duke! Vail your regard   20
    Upon a wrong'd—I would fain have said, a maid.
    O worthy prince, dishonour not your eye
    By throwing it on any other object,
    Till you have heard me in my true complaint,
    And given me justice, justice, justice, justice!   25

Duke   Relate your wrongs. In what? By whom? Be
        brief.
    Here is Lord Angelo shall give you justice;
    Reveal yourself to him.

Isabella   O worthy Duke,
    You bid me seek redemption of the devil!
    Hear me yourself: for that which I must speak   30
    Must either punish me, not being believed,
    Or wring redress from you. Hear me! O hear me,
        hear!

Angelo   My lord, her wits I fear me are not firm.
    She hath been a suitor to me for her brother
    Cut off by course of justice—

Isabella   By course of justice! 35

Angelo   And she will speak most bitterly and strange.

Isabella   Most strange, but yet most truly, will I speak.
    That Angelo's forsworn, is it not strange?

15–16. *That outward courtesies . . . within:* that the external signs of friendliness
   attempt to show my inner gratitude. *fain:* willingly.
20. *Vail your regard:* lower your glance.
21. *I would fain:* I wish I could.
31. *punish me:* result in my punishment.
32. *Or wring redress from you:* or force you to right my wrong.
38. *forsworn:* perjured.

	That Angelo's a murderer, is't not strange?	
	That Angelo is an adulterous thief,	40
	An hypocrite, a virgin-violator,	
	Is it not strange and strange?	

Duke   Nay, it is ten times strange.

Isabella   It is not truer he is Angelo,
Than this is all as true as it is strange;
Nay, it is ten times true, for truth is truth   45
To the end of reckoning.

Duke   Away with her: poor soul,
She speaks this in th'infirmity of sense.

Isabella   O prince, I conjure thee, as thou believest
There is another comfort than this world,
That thou neglect me not with that opinion   50
That I am touch'd with madness. Make not
        impossible
That which but seems unlike. 'Tis not impossible
But one, the wicked'st caitiff on the ground,
May seem as shy, as grave, as just, as absolute
As Angelo; even so may Angelo,   55
In all his dressings, characts, titles, forms,
Be an arch-villain. Believe it, royal prince,
If he be less, he's nothing; but he's more,
Had I more name for badness.

Duke   By mine honesty,
If she be mad, as I believe no other,   60

46. *To the end of reckoning:* always, absolutely.
47. *th'infirmity of sense:* weakness of mind.
48. *conjure thee:* call upon you solemnly.
49. *another comfort than this world:* i.e. Heaven.
50–1. *That thou . . . touch'd with madness:* that you do not ignore me by deciding that I am mad.
51–2. *Make not . . . unlike:* do not regard as impossible that which merely seems improbable.
53. *But:* but that.   *caitiff:* villain.
54. *absolute:* free from imperfection.
56. *dressings:* ornaments of office.   *characts:* insignia.   *forms:* manners.
59. *Had I more name for badness:* had I something worse to call him.

Her madness hath the oddest frame of sense,
Such a dependency of thing on thing,
As e'er I heard in madness.

Isabella   O gracious Duke,
Harp not on that; nor do not banish reason
For inequality; but let your reason serve   65
To make the truth appear where it seems hid,
And hide the false seems true.

Duke   Many that are not mad
Have, sure, more lack of reason. What would
    you say?

Isabella   I am the sister of one Claudio,
Condemn'd upon the act of fornication   70
To lose his head; condemn'd by Angelo.
I, in probation of a sisterhood,
Was sent to by my brother; one Lucio
As then the messenger—

Lucio   That's I, and 't like your Grace.
I came to her from Claudio, and desired her   75
To try her gracious fortune with Lord Angelo
For her poor brother's pardon.

Isabella   That's he indeed.

Duke   You were not bid to speak.

Lucio   No, my good lord;
Nor wish'd to hold my peace.

Duke   I wish you now, then;
Pray you, take note of it: and when you have   80

---

61. *frame of sense:* structure of reason.
62–3. *Such . . . heard in madness:* such a coherence and relevance as I have not
    heard spoken in madness.
64. *Harp not on that:* do not keep talking of my madness.
65. *inequality:* this may mean either Isabella's social inferiority to Angelo, or
    the discrepancy between her accusation and Angelo's reputation.
65–7. *but let . . . false seems true:* but use your reason to discover and make known
    the truth which is obscured and to cover the falsehood which now seems to
    be the truth.
72. *in probation of a sisterhood:* a novice in a religious order.
74. *As then:* being then.   *and 't like:* if it please.
79. *wish'd:* asked, bid.

	A business for yourself, pray heaven you then	
	Be perfect.	
Lucio	I warrant your honour.	
Duke	The warrant's for yourself: take heed to't.	
Isabella	This gentleman told somewhat of my tale—	
Lucio	Right.	85
Duke	It may be right, but you are i' th' wrong	
	To speak before your time. Proceed.	
Isabella	I went	
	To this pernicious caitiff Deputy—	
Duke	That's somewhat madly spoken.	
Isabella	Pardon it;	
	The phrase is to the matter.	90
Duke	Mended again. The matter: proceed.	
Isabella	In brief, to set the needless process by,	
	How I persuaded, how I pray'd and kneel'd,	
	How he refell'd me, and how I replied—	
	For this was of much length—the vile conclusion	95
	I now begin with grief and shame to utter.	
	He would not, but by gift of my chaste body	
	To his concupiscible intemperate lust,	
	Release my brother; and after much debatement,	
	My sisterly remorse confutes mine honour,	100
	And I did yield to him. But the next morn	
	betimes,	

81. *A business for yourself:* a case of your own.
82. *perfect:* fully prepared. *I warrant your honour:* I give you my assurance.
83. *warrant:* the Duke puns on the word, using it to mean 'order for arrest'.
84. *somewhat:* part.
88. *pernicious caitiff:* wicked villain.
89. *somewhat:* rather.
90. *to the matter:* relevant to my story.
91. *Mended again:* a withdrawal of the allegation that Isabella's description of Angelo was 'madly spoken'.
92. *to set the needless process by:* to set aside the insignificant part of my story.
94. *refell'd:* refuted.
98. *concupiscible:* libidinous, lascivious.
99. *debatement:* deliberation.
100. *remorse:* compassion. *confutes:* overcomes.
101. *betimes:* early.

<table>
<tr><td></td><td>His purpose surfeiting, he sends a warrant
For my poor brother's head.</td><td></td></tr>
<tr><td>*Duke*</td><td>   This is most likely!</td><td></td></tr>
<tr><td>*Isabella*</td><td>O, that it were as like as it is true.</td><td></td></tr>
<tr><td>*Duke*</td><td>By heaven, fond wretch, thou know'st not what
    thou speak'st,</td><td>105</td></tr>
</table>

By heaven, fond wretch, thou know'st not what
    thou speak'st,   105
Or else thou art suborn'd against his honour
In hateful practice. First, his integrity
Stands without blemish; next, it imports no
    reason
That with such vehemency he should pursue
Faults proper to himself. If he had so offended,   110
He would have weigh'd thy brother by himself,
And not have cut him off. Some one hath set you
    on:
Confess the truth, and say by whose advice
Thou cam'st here to complain.

Isabella   And is this all?

Then, O you blessed ministers above,   115
Keep me in patience, and with ripen'd time
Unfold the evil which is here wrapt up
In countenance! Heaven shield your Grace from
    woe,
As I, thus wrong'd, hence unbelievèd go.

---

102. *His purpose surfeiting:* having glutted his desire.   *warrant:* order.
104. *like:* probable.
105. *fond:* foolish.
106. *suborn'd:* bribed to give false witness.   *his honour:* Angelo's reputation.
107. *In hateful practice:* as part of a wicked plot.
108–10. *it imports . . . Faults proper to himself:* there would be no sense in Angelo's punishing so vigorously faults which he had himself.
108. *imports:* implies.
110–12. *If he had . . . cut him off:* if he had been guilty of this, he would have judged Claudio's offence in the light of his own and would not have had him executed.
112. *set you on:* incited you.
115. *ministers:* angels.
117–18. *Unfold . . . In countenance:* reveal the wickedness which is concealed by Angelo's outward bearing. 'In countenance' also means 'given general approval'.

Duke	I know you'd fain be gone. An officer! 120
	(ISABELLA *is arrested*).
	To prison with her! Shall we thus permit
	A blasting and a scandalous breath to fall
	On him so near us? This needs must be a practice.
	Who knew of your intent and coming hither?
Isabella	One that I would were here, Friar Lodowick. 125
Duke	A ghostly father, belike. Who knows that
	Lodowick?
Lucio	My lord, I know him; 'tis a meddling friar;
	I do not like the man; had he been lay, my lord,
	For certain words he spake against your Grace
	In your retirement, I had swinged him soundly. 130
Duke	Words against me? This's a good friar, belike!
	And to set on this wretched woman here
	Against our substitute! Let this friar be found.
Lucio	But yesternight, my lord, she and that friar,
	I saw them at the prison: a saucy friar, 135
	A very scurvy fellow.
Friar Peter	Blessed be your royal Grace!
	I have stood by, my lord, and I have heard
	Your royal ear abused. First hath this woman
	Most wrongfully accused your substitute, 140
	Who is as free from touch or soil with her
	As she from one ungot.
Duke	We did believe no less.
	Know you that Friar Lodowick that she speaks of?
Friar Peter	I know him for a man divine and holy,

120. *fain:* willingly, gladly.
122. *blasting:* withering.
123. *This needs must be a practice:* this is undoubtedly a plot.
126. *ghostly:* spiritual.   *belike:* probably.
128. *lay:* secular.
130. *your retirement:* the period when you were away.   *swinged:* beaten.
131. *belike:* doubtless.
135. *saucy:* wanton, impudent.
136. *scurvy:* disgusting.
141. *touch or soil:* sexual contact.
142. *one ungot:* someone not yet conceived.

	Not scurvy, nor a temporary meddler,	145
	As he's reported by this gentleman;	
	And, on my trust, a man that never yet	
	Did, as he vouches, misreport your Grace.	
Lucio	My lord, most villainously; believe it.	
Friar Peter	Well, he in time may come to clear himself;	150
	But at this instant he is sick, my lord,	
	Of a strange fever. Upon his mere request—	
	Being come to knowledge that there was complaint	
	Intended 'gainst Lord Angelo—came I hither,	
	To speak, as from his mouth, what he doth know	155
	Is true and false; and what he with his oath	
	And all probation will make up full clear	
	Whensoever he's convented. First, for this woman,	
	To justify this worthy nobleman	
	So vulgarly and personally accused,	160
	Her shall you hear disprovèd to her eyes,	
	Till she herself confess it.	
Duke	Good friar, let's hear it.	

(ISABELLA *is led off, guarded, and* MARIANA *comes*
forward, still veiled

Do you not smile at this, Lord Angelo?
O heaven, the vanity of wretched fools!
Give us some seats. Come, cousin Angelo, 165
In this I'll be impartial: be you judge
Of your own cause. Is this the witness, friar?

145. *a temporary meddler:* one who meddles with worldly affairs.
148. *as he vouches:* as Lucio maintains. *misreport:* slander.
152. *mere:* absolute, direct.
157. *probation:* proof.
158. *convented:* summoned. *for this woman:* as far as Isabella is concerned.
159. *justify:* vindicate.
160. *vulgarly:* publicly.
161. *to her eyes:* to her face.
164. *vanity:* illusion.
166. *I'll be impartial:* I'll take no side.

	First, let her show her face, and after, speak.	
Mariana	Pardon, my lord; I will not show my face	
	Until my husband bid me.	170
Duke	What, are you married?	
Mariana	No, my lord.	
Duke	Are you a maid?	
Mariana	No, my lord.	
Duke	A widow, then?	175
Mariana	Neither, my lord.	
Duke	Why, you are nothing, then: neither maid, widow, nor wife?	
Lucio	My lord, she may be a punk; for many of them are neither maid, widow, nor wife.	180
Duke	Silence that fellow: I would he had some cause To prattle for himself.	
Lucio	Well, my lord.	
Mariana	My lord, I do confess I ne'er was married; And I confess, besides, I am no maid. I have known my husband; yet my husband Knows not that ever he knew me.	185
Lucio	He was drunk, then, my lord: it can be no better.	
Duke	For the benefit of silence, would thou wert so too!	190
Lucio	Well, my lord.	
Duke	This is no witness for Lord Angelo.	
Mariana	Now I come to't, my lord. She that accuses him of fornication, In self-same manner doth accuse my husband, And charges him, my lord, with such a time When I'll depose I had him in mine arms	195

179. *punk:* prostitute.
186–7. *known:* throughout this passage there is play on the sexual meaning of the verb 'to know'.
195. *In self-same manner:* similarly.
196–8. *And charges . . . th'effect of love:* and accuses him of being with her at the very time when I will swear that he was in my arms making love to me.
197. *depose:* give on oath.

	With all th'effect of love.	
Angelo	Charges she moe than me?	
Mariana	Not that I know.	
Duke	No? You say your husband.	200
Mariana	Why, just, my lord, and that is Angelo,	
	Who thinks he knows that he ne'er knew my body,	
	But knows, he thinks, that he knows Isabel's.	
Angelo	This is a strange abuse. Let's see thy face.	
Mariana	My husband bids me; now I will unmask.	205

(Unveiling

	This is that face, thou cruel Angelo,	
	Which once thou swor'st was worth the looking on;	
	This is the hand which, with a vow'd contráct,	
	Was fast belock'd in thine; this is the body	
	That took away the match from Isabel,	210
	And did supply thee at thy garden-house	
	In her imagined person.	
Duke	Know you this woman?	
Lucio	Carnally, she says.	
Duke	Sirrah, no more!	
Lucio	Enough, my lord.	
Angelo	My lord, I must confess I know this woman;	215
	And five years since there was some speech of marriage	
	Betwixt myself and her; which was broke off,	
	Partly for that her promisèd proportions	
	Came short of composition; but in chief	

198. *effect:* manifestation, fulfilment.
199. *moe:* more, i.e. anyone else.
201. *just:* exactly.
204 *abuse:* slander.
209. *fast belock'd:* firmly clasped.
210. *match:* assignation.
211. *supply thee:* satisfy your lust.
218–19. *for that . . . short of composition:* because her dowry was less than that agreed.

For that her reputation was disvalued   220
In levity: since which time of five years
I never spake with her, saw her, nor heard from
    her,
Upon my faith and honour.

Mariana   Noble prince,
As there comes light from heaven, and words from
    breath,
As there is sense in truth, and truth in virtue,   225
I am affianced this man's wife as strongly
As words could make up vows: and, my good
    lord,
But Tuesday night last gone, in's garden-house
He knew me as a wife. As this is true,
Let me in safety raise me from my knees,   230
Or else for ever be confixèd here,
A marble monument!

Angelo   I did but smile till now:
Now, good my lord, give me the scope of justice;
My patience here is touch'd. I do perceive
These poor informal women are no more   235
But instruments of some more mightier member
That sets them on: let me have way, my lord,
To find this practice out.

Duke   Ay, with my heart;
And punish them to your height of pleasure.
Thou foolish friar, and thou pernicious woman,   240

220–1. *For that . . . In levity:* because her reputation was destroyed by her loose
    morality.
225. *sense:* reason.
226. *affianced this man's wife:* betrothed to this man.
231. *confixèd:* firmly fixed.
233. *scope:* freedom, cf. I, i, 65.
234. *touch'd:* tried.
235. *informal:* crazy, disordered.
236. *member:* person.
240. *pernicious:* wicked.

Compact with her that's gone, think'st thou thy
    oaths,
Though they would swear down each particular
    saint,
Were testimonies against his worth and credit,
That's seal'd in approbation? You, Lord Escalus,
Sit with my cousin; lend him your kind pains   245
To find out this abuse, whence 'tis derived.
There is another friar that set them on;
Let him be sent for.

Friar Peter   Would he were here, my lord, for he indeed
Hath set the women on to this complaint.   250
Your provost knows the place where he abides,
And he may fetch him.

Duke   Go, do it instantly.
                           (*Exit Provost*
And you, my noble and well-warranted cousin,
Whom it concerns to hear this matter forth,
Do with your injuries as seems you best   255
In any chastisement; I for a while will leave you;
But stir not you till you have well determined
Upon these slanderers.

Escalus   My lord, we'll do it throughly.   (*Exit Duke*
Signior Lucio, did not you say you knew that 260
Friar Lodowick to be a dishonest person?

Lucio   'Cucullus non facit monachum'; honest in nothing

241. *Compact:* in league. *her that's gone:* i.e. Isabella.
241-4. *think'st thou . . . seal'd in approbation:* do you think that your oaths, even
    if they could bring down each saint by whom you swear, would be evidence
    against a man whose merit and reputation have been confirmed by proof?
245-6. *lend him . . . derived:* give him your assistance to uncover the source of
    this corruption.
253. *well-warranted:* well-tested, but the word 'warrant' is used ironically; cf. l. 83.
254. *Whom . . . forth:* who are personally involved in hearing the rest of this case.
255-6. *Do . . . In any chastisement:* deal out punishment for the slander you have
    suffered as you see fit.
257. *determined:* passed judgment.
262. *'Cucullus non facit monachum':* the cowl does not make the monk. A proverb
    expressing the theme that appearances can be misleading. It is ironic since
    Lucio is indeed taken in by the Duke's disguising cowl.

	but in his clothes, and one that hath spoke most villainous speeches of the Duke.
Escalus	We shall entreat you to abide here till he come, 265 and enforce them against him. We shall find this friar a notable fellow.
Lucio	As any in Vienna, on my word.
Escalus	Call that same Isabel here once again, I would speak with her. (*Exit an Attendant*) Pray you, my 270 lord, give me leave to question; you shall see how I'll handle her.
Lucio	Not better than he, by her own report.
Escalus	Say you?
Lucio	Marry, sir, I think if you handled her privately 275 she would sooner confess; perchance publicly she'll be ashamed.
Escalus	I will go darkly to work with her.
Lucio	That's the way; for women are light at midnight.

Enter ISABELLA *still under arrest, followed by the* DUKE *disguised as a Friar, and the* PROVOST

Escalus	Come on, mistress, here's a gentlewoman denies 280 all that you have said.
Lucio	My lord, here comes the rascal I spoke of, here with the provost.
Escalus	In very good time. Speak not you to him till we call upon you. 285
Lucio	Mum.
Escalus	Come, sir: did you set these women on to slander Lord Angelo? They have confessed you did.
Duke	'Tis false. 290

266. *enforce them against him*: strongly charge him with them.
267. *notable*: notorious, infamous.
273. *Not . . . report*: Lucio finds a sexual innuendo in the word 'handle'.
278. *darkly*: secretly; Lucio takes the meaning 'in the dark'.
279. *light*: wanton, unchaste.
286. *Mum*: silent.

Escalus	How! Know you where you are?
Duke	Respect to your great place; and let the devil
	Be sometime honour'd for his burning throne.
	Where is the Duke? 'Tis he should hear me
	speak.
Escalus	The Duke's in us; and we will hear you speak; 295
	Look you speak justly.
Duke	Boldly, at least. But, O, poor souls,
	Come you to seek the lamb here of the fox?
	Goodnight to your redress! Is the Duke gone?
	Then is your cause gone too. The Duke's unjust, 300
	Thus to retort your manifest appeal,
	And put your trial in the villain's mouth
	Which here you come to accuse.
Lucio	This is the rascal: this is he I spoke of.
Escalus	Why, thou unreverend and unhallow'd friar; 305
	Is't not enough thou hast suborn'd these women
	To accuse this worthy man, but in foul mouth,
	And in the witness of his proper ear,
	To call him villain? And then to glance from him
	To th'Duke himself, to tax him with injustice? 310
	Take him hence; to the rack with him! We'll
	touse you
	Joint by joint, but we will know his purpose.

292–3. *and let the devil . . . burning throne:* even the devil should be respected because of his position of authority. The Duke's sarcastic comment refers, of course, to Angelo.

295. *The Duke's in us:* we represent the Duke's authority.

298. *Come you to seek the lamb here of the fox:* a line echoing Matthew, vii, 15: 'Beware of false prophets, which come to you in sheep's clothing, but inwardly they are ravening wolves.'

299. *Goodnight to your redress:* this is the end of your hope for reparation.

301. *retort:* reject. *manifest appeal:* well substantiated accusation.

305. *unreverend:* irreverent. *unhallow'd:* unholy.

306. *suborn'd:* corrupted, bribed.

307. *in foul mouth:* with grossly abusive words.

308. *in the witness of his proper ear:* in his own hearing.

309. *to glance:* to pass quickly.

310. *tax:* accuse.

311. *touse:* tear.

312. *but:* only. *his purpose:* the reason for his slandering Angelo.

	What! Unjust!	
Duke	Be not so hot; the Duke	
	Dare no more stretch this finger of mine than he	
	Dare rack his own: his subject am I not,	315
	Nor here provincial. My business in this state	
	Made me a looker-on here in Vienna,	
	Where I have seen corruption boil and bubble	
	Till it o'er-run the stew: laws for all faults,	
	But faults so countenanced, that the strong statutes	320
	Stand like the forfeits in a barber's shop,	
	As much in mock as mark.	
Escalus	Slander to the state! Away with him to prison!	
Angelo	What can you vouch against him, Signior Lucio?	
	Is this the man that you did tell us of?	325
Lucio	'Tis he, my lord. Come hither, goodman bald-pate; do you know me?	
Duke	I remember you, sir, by the sound of your voice; I met you at the prison, in the absence of the Duke.	
Lucio	O, did you so? And do you remember what you said of the Duke?	330
Duke	Most notedly, sir.	
Lucio	Do you so, sir? And was the Duke a fleshmonger, a fool, and a coward, as you then reported him to be?	335

313. *hot:* passionate.
316. *provincial:* subject to the local laws.
319. *stew:* cauldron. But there is also a pun on the second meaning, 'brothel'.
320. *countenanced:* sanctioned.   *strong statutes:* stern laws.
321. *forfeits in a barber's shop:* barbers were also surgeons, and it was apparently a custom to hang up in their shops a list of mock penalties (such as tooth extraction and other amputations) to be imposed on customers who swore or misbehaved.
322. *mark:* warning, deterrent.
324. *vouch:* testify.
326. *goodman:* a form of address used for people below the rank of gentleman. *baldpate:* referring to the Friar's tonsure.
332. *notedly:* particularly.
333. *fleshmonger:* fornicator.

Duke	You must, sir, change persons with me, ere you make that my report. *You* indeed spoke so of him, and much more, much worse.
Lucio	O, thou damnable fellow! Did not I pluck thee by the nose for thy speeches? 340
Duke	I protest I love the Duke as I love myself.
Angelo	Hark how the villain would close now, after his treasonable abuses!
Escalus	Such a fellow is not to be talked withal. Away with him to prison! Where is the provost? Away 345 with him to prison; lay bolts enough upon him: let him speak no more. Away with those giglets too, and with the other confederate companion!
Duke	(*To the Provost*) Stay, sir, stay awhile.
Angelo	What, resists he? Help him, Lucio. 350
Lucio	Come, sir; come, sir; come, sir; foh, sir! Why, you bald-pated, lying rascal, you must be hooded, must you? Show your knave's visage, with a pox to you! Show your sheep-biting face, and be hanged an hour! Will't not off? 355

(*Pulls off the friar's hood, and discovers the Duke*

Duke	Thou art the first knave that e'er madest a Duke. First, provost, let me bail these gentle three. (*To Lucio*) Sneak not away, sir, for the friar and you Must have a word anon. Lay hold on him.
Lucio	This may prove worse than hanging. 360

342. *close:* retract.
344. *withal:* with.
347. *giglets:* loose women.
348. *the other confederate companion:* i.e. Friar Peter.
353. *pox:* curse.
354–5. *sheep-biting:* wolvish. Cf. V, i, 298.   *hanged an hour:* hanging was the traditional punishment for sheep stealing. The malefactor would hang for an hour before being officially pronounced dead.
357. *bail:* liberate.
359. *anon:* soon.

Duke	(*To Escalus*) What you have spoke I pardon: sit you down.
	We'll borrow place of him. (*To Angelo*) Sir, by your leave.
	Hast thou or word, or wit, or impudence,
	That yet can do thee office? If thou hast
	Rely upon it till my tale be heard, 365
	And hold no longer out.
Angelo	O my dread lord,
	I should be guiltier than my guiltiness,
	To think I can be undiscernible,
	When I perceive your Grace, like power divine,
	Hath look'd upon my passes. Then, good prince, 370
	No longer session hold upon my shame,
	But let my trial be mine own confession:
	Immediate sentence then, and sequent death,
	Is all the grace I beg.
Duke	Come hither, Mariana.
	Say, wast thou e'er contracted to this woman? 375
Angelo	I was, my lord.
Duke	Go take her hence, and marry her instantly.
	Do you the office, friar; which consummate,
	Return him here again. Go with him, provost.

(*Exeunt Angelo, Mariana, Friar Peter and Provost*

362. *We'll borrow place of him*: I will change places with Angelo. The Duke continues to conduct the trial with Angelo now the accused.
363. *wit*: invention.
364. *That yet can do thee office*: that can now be of assistance to you.
365-6. *Rely . . . hold no longer out*: hold on to your excuse until you have heard my story, and then give up.
366. *dread*: dreaded and revered.
368. *be undiscernible*: escape detection.
370. *passes*: contrivances.
371. *No longer session hold upon my shame*: do not continue with formal investigation of my disgrace.
373. *sequent*: consequent, following.
374. *grace*: favour.
375. *contracted*: betrothed.
378. *which consummate*: when it is concluded.

Escalus	My lord, I am more amazed at his dishonour 380
	Than at the strangeness of it.
Duke	Come hither, Isabel.

Your friar is now your prince. As I was then
Advértising and holy to your business,
Not changing heart with habit, I am still
Attorney'd at your service.

Isabella   O give me pardon,   385
That I, your vassal, have employ'd and pain'd
Your unknown sovereignty!

Duke   You are pardon'd, Isabel.
And now, dear maid, be you as free to us.
Your brother's death, I know, sits at your heart;
And you may marvel why I obscured myself,   390
Labouring to save his life, and would not rather
Make rash remonstrance of my hidden power
Than let him so be lost. O most kind maid,
It was the swift celerity of his death,
Which I did think with slower foot came on,   395
That brain'd my purpose. But peace be with him!
That life is better life, past fearing death,
Than that which lives to fear: make it your
   comfort,

380–1. *My lord . . . strangeness of it:* I am more astounded by the fact that Angelo
   is guilty than by the remarkable way in which his guilt has been proved.
383. *Advértising:* attentive.   *holy:* devoted.
384. *Not changing heart with habit:* not altering my disposition with my change of
   clothes.
385. *Attorney'd at your service:* an agent acting on your behalf.
386. *vassal:* subject.   *pain'd:* put to trouble.
388. *be you as free to us:* forgive me as I have forgiven you.   *free:* generous,
   magnanimous.
389. *sits at your heart:* lies heavy on your heart.
390. *obscured myself:* kept my authority hidden.
392. *rash remonstrance:* immediate demonstration.
393. *kind:* loving. 'Kind' implies the strong natural affection of kinship.
394. *celerity:* speed.
395. *with slower foot came on:* would happen less suddenly.
396. *brain'd:* defeated.
398–9. *make it . . . brother:* take consolation in the knowledge that your brother is
   happier being dead.

So happy is your brother.

Isabella   I do, my lord.

Re-enter ANGELO, MARIANA, FRIAR PETER, *and* PROVOST

Duke   For this new-married man approaching here,   400
Whose salt imagination yet hath wrong'd
Your well-defended honour, you must pardon
For Mariana's sake: but as he adjudged your
    brother—
Being criminal in double violation
Of sacred chastity and of promise-breach   405
Thereon dependent—for your brother's life
The very mercy of the law cries out
Most audible, even from his proper tongue,
'An Angelo for Claudio, death for death!'
Haste still pays haste, and leisure answers leisure;   410
Like doth quit like, and Measure still for Measure.
Then, Angelo, thy fault's thus manifested;
Which, though thou wouldst deny, denies thee
    vantage.
We do condemn thee to the very block
Where Claudio stoop'd to death, and with like
    haste.   415
Away with him!

Mariana   O my most gracious lord,
I hope you will not mock me with a husband.

Duke   It is your husband mock'd you with a husband.
Consenting to the safeguard of your honour,

401-2. *Whose salt imagination . . . honour:* who has, in his lecherous imagination,
    violated your well-defended chastity.
403. *adjudged:* condemned.
405-6. *promise-breach Thereon dependent:* Angelo's second crime of violation was the
    breaking of the promise he had made to spare Claudio's life. This was de-
    pendent on his first, intended, violation of Isabella's chastity.
407. *The very mercy of the law:* the law, even at its most merciful.
408. *audible:* audibly.
410-11. *'Haste . . . Measure still for Measure:* See *Introduction, p.* 37.
412-13. *thy fault's . . . denies thee vantage:* even if you wished to deny it, your
    offence is so blatant that you would not be given the opportunity.

	I thought your marriage fit; else imputation, 420
	For that he knew you, might reproach your life
	And choke your good to come. For his posses-
	sions,
	Although by confiscation they are ours,
	We do instate and widow you withal,
	To buy you a better husband.
Mariana	O my dear lord, 425
	I crave no other, nor no better man.
Duke	Never crave him; we are definitive.
Mariana	Gentle my liege— (*Kneeling*
Duke	You do but lose your labour.
	Away with him to death! (*To Lucio*) Now sir, to
	you.
Mariana	O my good lord! Sweet Isabel, take my part; 430
	Lend me your knees, and all my life to come
	I'll lend you all my life to do you service.
Duke	Against all sense you do importune her:
	Should she kneel down in mercy of this fact,
	Her brother's ghost his pavèd bed would break, 435
	And take her hence in horror.
Mariana	Isabel,
	Sweet Isabel, do yet but kneel by me;
	Hold up your hands, say nothing: I'll speak all.
	They say best men are moulded out of faults,
	And, for the most, become much more the better 440

420. *fit:* proper, appropriate.
420-22. *else imputation . . . good to come:* otherwise your being reputed to have had intercourse with Angelo might bring disgrace on your life and destroy your future happiness.
420. *imputation:* ill repute.
422. *For:* as for.
424. *instate:* endow. *widow:* give as a settlement on widowhood.
427. *definitive:* resolute.
428. *You do but lose your labour:* you are merely wasting your efforts.
431. *Lend me your knees:* kneel down and plead with me.
433. *sense:* reason, natural feeling. *importune:* beseech, trouble.
434. *in mercy of this fact:* to ask mercy for this evil deed.
435. *pavèd bed:* tomb.
440. *for the most:* for the most part.

For being a little bad: so may my husband.
O Isabel, will you not lend a knee?

Duke He dies for Claudio's death.

Isabella   Most bounteous sir, *(Kneeling*
Look, if it please you, on this man condemn'd,
As if my brother lived: I partly think   •   445
A due sincerity govern'd his deeds,
Till he did look on me. Since it is so,
Let him not die. My brother had but justice,
In that he did the thing for which he died:
For Angelo,   450
His act did not o'ertake his bad intent,
And must be buried but as an intent
That perish'd by the way. Thoughts are no
    subjects;
Intents, but merely thoughts.

Mariana   Merely, my lord.

Duke Your suit's unprofitable. Stand up, I say.   455
I have bethought me of another fault.
Provost, how came it Claudio was beheaded
At an unusual hour?

Provost   It was commanded so.

Duke Had you a special warrant for the deed?

Provost No, my good lord: it was by private message. 460

Duke For which I do discharge you of your office.
Give up your keys.

Provost   Pardon me, noble lord:
I thought it was a fault, but knew it not;
Yet did repent me after more advice;

443. *bounteous:* generous.
446. *due:* proper, fitting.
451. *His act . . . intent:* he did not actually achieve his evil purpose.
453–4. *Thoughts are . . . merely thoughts:* thoughts cannot be controlled by law;
    intentions are no more than thoughts.
454. *Merely:* absolutely.
455. *Your suit's unprofitable:* your pleading is futile.
456. *bethought me:* thought.
459. *warrant:* order.
464. *advice:* reflection.

| | For testimony whereof, one in the prison, | 465 |

	For testimony whereof, one in the prison,	465
	That should by private order else have died,	
	I have reserved alive.	
Duke	What's he?	
Provost	His name is Barnardine.	
Duke	I would thou hadst done so by Claudio.	
	Go fetch him hither; let me look upon him.	
	(*Exit Provost*	

Escalus	I am sorry one so learned and so wise	470
	As you, Lord Angelo, have still appear'd,	
	Should slip so grossly, both in the heat of blood	
	And lack of temper'd judgement afterward.	
Angelo	I am sorry that such sorrow I procure,	
	And so deep sticks it in my penitent heart,	475
	That I crave death more willingly than mercy;	
	'Tis my deserving, and I do entreat it.	

Re-enter PROVOST, *with* BARNARDINE, CLAUDIO *muffled, and* JULIET

Duke	Which is that Barnardine?	
Provost	This, my lord.	
Duke	There was a friar told me of this man.	
	Sirrah, thou art said to have a stubborn soul	480
	That apprehends no further than this world,	
	And squar'st thy life according. Thou'rt con-	
	demn'd;	
	But, for those earthly faults, I quit them all,	
	And pray thee take this mercy to provide	
	For better times to come. Friar, advise him;	485

465. *testimony:* witness.
471. *still:* always.
472. *slip so grossly:* transgress so blatantly and coarsely. *blood:* passion.
473. *temper'd:* considered.
474. *procure:* bring about.
481. *apprehends:* imagines.
482. *squar'st:* regulate.
483. *quit:* remit.
485. *advise:* counsel.

I leave him to your hand. What muffled fellow's
    that?

Provost This is another prisoner that I saved,
Who should have died when Claudio lost his
    head;
As like almost to Claudio as himself.

                             (*Unmuffles Claudio*

Duke (*To Isabella*) If he be like your brother, for his sake 490
Is he pardon'd; and, for your lovely sake,
Give me your hand, and say you will be mine,
He is my brother too: but fitter time for that.
By this Lord Angelo perceives he's safe;
Methinks I see a quickening in his eye.   495
Well, Angelo, your evil quits you well.
Look that you love your wife; her worth, worth
    yours.
I find an apt remission in myself:
And yet here's one in place I cannot pardon.
(*To Lucio*) You, sirrah, that knew me for a fool,
    a coward,   500
One all of luxury, an ass, a madman:
Wherein have I so deserved of you
That you extol me thus?

Lucio 'Faith, my lord, I spoke it but according to the
trick: if you will hang me for it, you may: but I 505
had rather it would please you I might be whipt.

Duke Whipt first, sir, and hang'd after.
Proclaim it, provost, round about the city,

---

495. *a quickening:* a return of life.
496. *quits:* rewards, repays.
497. *her worth, worth yours:* that your deserving measures up to hers.
498. *an apt remission:* a readiness to forgive.
499. *in place:* at hand.
501. *luxury:* lust.
503. *extol:* praise.
504–5. *according to the trick:* out of habit.

If any woman wrong'd by this lewd fellow—
As I have heard him swear himself there's one   510
Whom he begot with child—let her appear,
And he shall marry her: the nuptial finish'd,
Let him be whipt and hang'd.

Lucio   I beseech your highness, do not marry me to a
whore. Your highness said even now, I made you 515
a Duke: good my lord, do not recompense me
in making me a cuckold.

Duke   Upon mine honour thou shalt marry her.
Thy slanders I forgive, and therewithal
Remit thy other forfeits. Take him to prison.   520
And see our pleasure herein executed.

Lucio   Marrying a punk, my lord, is pressing to death,
whipping, and hanging.

Duke   Slandering a prince deserves it.

                          (*Exeunt Officers with Lucio*

She, Claudio, that you wrong'd, look you restore. 525
Joy to you, Mariana; love her, Angelo:
I have confess'd her, and I know her virtue.
Thanks, good friend Escalus, for thy much
    goodness:
There's more behind that is more gratulate.
Thanks, provost, for thy care and secrecy: 530
We shall employ thee in a worthier place.
Forgive him, Angelo, that brought you home
The head of Ragozine for Claudio's:
The offence pardons itself. Dear Isabel,
I have a motion much imports your good;   535
Whereto if you'll a willing ear incline,

---

509. *lewd:* worthless, vile.
512. *nuptial:* wedding.
519. *therewithal:* at the same time.
522. *punk:* whore. *pressing to death:* an ancient torture.
525. *She . . . restore:* i.e. marry Julietta.
529. *There's . . . gratulate:* further reward is to come. *gratulate:* gratifying.
535. *a motion much imports your good:* a proposal to your advantage.

What's mine is yours, and what is yours is mine.
So bring us to our palace; where we'll show
What's yet behind, that's meet you all should
know.   (*Exeunt*

538. *bring:* accompany.
539. *What's yet behind:* what has not yet been revealed.   *meet:* fitting, proper.

COMMENTARY

1 Shakespeare's Source

Shakespeare's principal source was *The History of Promos and Cassandra*, a play written by George Whetstone in 1578. This play is divided into two parts and the plot is briefly as follows:

In the city of Julio, ruled over by the King of Hungary, Lord Promos, a newly appointed magistrate, revives a law which enables him to sentence to death Andrugio, a young man guilty of fornication. At Andrugio's request Cassandra, his chaste and beautiful sister, pleads for his life. Promos promises to grant it on condition that she sleeps with him. Cassandra at first refuses but is persuaded by Andrugio to yield to Promos on condition that he promises to marry her. Once his lust is satisfied, Promos instructs Andrugio's gaoler to execute him and to send his head to Cassandra. However, the gaoler is moved by God to free Andrugio and to send Cassandra the head of a recently executed felon.

In the second half of the play Cassandra determines to reveal her shame to the King of Hungary and to plead to him for justice. He visits the city and on discovering that Promos is guilty he pronounces that he must marry Cassandra and then be executed. Once married, Cassandra finds that she loves Promos and proceeds to plead for his life. The King refuses to grant it until Andrugio, who is present in disguise, reveals that he is still alive, whereupon both he and Promos are pardoned.

To Whetstone's plot Shakespeare made two major alterations:

1. He greatly enlarged the part of the King, who as the Duke in *Measure for Measure* controls the entire action. The idea of a ruler taking on a disguise and moving among his people has its origins in legend. It was popular with Elizabethan and Jacobean dramatists (notable plays in which it is used include Marston's *The Malconten* and Middleton's *Phoenix*) and Shakespeare had himself used it in *King Henry V.*

2. He divided the part of Cassandra between two women, Isabella

and Mariana, thereby enabling Isabella to retain her virginity. Elizabethan audiences were familiar with the dramatic device of the 'bedtrick' (a device also used by Shakespeare in *All's Well that Ends Well*) and accepted as a convention the underlying idea that a man might sleep with one woman while thinking that she was another.

2 The Text of 'Measure for Measure'

Measure for Measure was first printed in the First Folio of 1623, seven years after Shakespeare's death. It is now generally believed that the text was set up in print by four compositors working from a transcript made from Shakespeare's 'foul papers', a term used by the Elizabethans to describe an author's own manuscript. The text is marred by a few omissions and inconsistencies. The omissions (cf. I, i, 8–9 and III, ii, 276–9) almost certainly resulted from the carelessness of the scrivener (thought to be Ralph Crane) who prepared the transcript or the compositors who worked on it in the printing house. The inconsistencies (cf. I, ii, 163 and I, iii, 21) are typical of an author working on major themes but unconcerned with the kind of minor details which could have been corrected when the theatre 'prompt book', or acting version, was constructed from the 'foul papers'.

3 Scene Localities

Editors generally describe Shakespeare's scene localities in some detail. The opening scene of *Measure for Measure* used to be located in 'an apartment in the Duke's palace'. More recently it has been suggested that the Duke is taking a private leave and that he should be dressed for travel. But Elizabethan staging did not allow for such nice distinctions. Shakespeare's settings are created by his characters and, since the Duke's character can be taken at different levels, the opening scene might be thought of as either a real leave-taking or a symbolic withdrawal of authority. The bareness of the Elizabethan stage would have allowed for both interpretations. Where a more specific setting is required the entry of a nun or a friar will, where necessary, change the stage to a nunnery or a monastery.

4 The Parable of the Talents, I, i, 33–41

This passage contains several oblique biblical allusions, including Luke, viii, 16; Mark, iv, 21 and Matthew, v, 14–16. Its chief inspiration, however, is the parable of the talents (Matthew, xxv, 14–30). The Duke, who resembles the Master in the parable in that he is distributing his powers before going on a journey, tells Angelo that virtues are Heaven-sent, and that if they are not used it is as though we did not have them. The greater the virtue, the greater the need to use it actively. Even small portions of Nature's excellence are only borrowed and she expects to be glorified by the good use made of them. (cf. Sonnet 4.)

5 Coining Images

One of several reasons why Angelo is called Angelo is that, like the coin, the 'angel', he receives the stamp of his sovereign. In the play there are a number of minting images. The verb 'to coin' could mean both 'to print coins' and 'to procreate' and both Angelo (II, iv, 45–9) and Isabella (II, iv, 130) compare counterfeiting to sex outside marriage.

6 The Duke and King James, I, i, 68–73 and II, iv, 24–30

Both these passages are thought to allude to King James I's avowed dislike of publicity. *Measure for Measure* was one of the first of Shakespeare's plays to be acted at King James's court and it is probable that as the temporal and spiritual leader of his people he would have seen the character of Duke Vincentio as a flattering portrait of himself. Shakespeare's company was financially dependent on both royal patronage and money earned by public performance. Shortly after James's accession to the English throne the company became 'the King's Men' and at least one other play, *Macbeth*, was written to please and flatter the Scottish king.

7 Act I, Scene, ii, lines 1–15

Having already heard the contents of Angelo's proclamation, Lucio and his two friends are putting on a show of bravado. The topical significance of some of their comments might now be lost to us but, since their nervous tension finds expression in elaborate verbal play revealing an obsession with sex and disease, the following glossary is included to augment the notes by showing some possible allusions.

l. 2 *Hungary*: 'hungry' could mean 'avidly amorous', cf. *Antony and Cleopatra*, II, ii, 242; l. 10 *steal*: pronounced like 'stale' which with *meat*, l. 15, was a slang term for prostitute; l. 13 *function*: could also mean 'sexual performance', cf. *Othello*, II, iii, 354; l. 14 *soldier*: virile man, cf. *Much Ado about Nothing*, I, i, 54; l. 15 *relish*: to savour, often used with sexual connotations.

8 Act I, Scene ii, line 2

composition: Lucio assumes that the Duke has gone away to negotiate a peace. This may be a topical allusion to King James I's endeavours to negotiate a settlement with Spain early in 1604.

9 Act I, scene ii, lines 77-9

Thus . . . custom-shrunk: These lines would have made it clear to the audience that the Vienna of the action was really a transparently disguised London. Early in 1604 England was at war with Spain, there was a major outbreak of plague in London, and treason trials and executions were taking place in Winchester.

10 Elizabethan Marriage Contracts

In Elizabethan England there were two sorts of betrothal. If a couple swore that they took each other in marriage their oath was legally binding but the Church required that they should be married in a church before they could live together as man and wife. This was *sponsalia per verba de praesenti* and is the kind of betrothal by which Claudio and Julietta were secretly joined. Angelo and Mariana had undergone a *sponsalia per verba de futuro*: a couple who became engaged by the terms of this kind of contract undertook to become husband and wife at a future date. Such a contract was not legally binding, but if it could be proved that cohabitation had taken place between the couple, a *de futuro* contract became as binding as a *de praesenti* contract. Thus by trapping Angelo into sleeping with Mariana the Duke ensures that he is legally married to her.

11 Act I, scene iii, lines 1–6

No, holy father ... Of burning youth: Friar Thomas has apparently assumed that the Duke requires shelter to enable him to conduct a secret love affair. The assumption is significant for two reasons: it develops the idea of Vienna as a city caught in the grip of lust, and it shows that the Duke, unlike Angelo, has not won for himself a virtuous reputation.

12 Puritans

The Puritans were a party of English protestants who considered that the Church of England had not been sufficiently 'purified' from the taint of Roman Catholicism. They were renowned for their moral strictness and Puritan extremists believed that a strict moral code could be enforced by law, several advocating the death penalty for sexual offences. One of these 'reformers', Phillip Stubbes, wrote a book called *The Anatomie of Abuses* (1583) in which he made a violent attack on the 'theaters and vncleane assemblies' which he considered lured people away from the churches. Stubbes and other Puritan writers urged that the theatres should be closed but, since the leading companies were patronized by Royalty, it was not until Cromwell came into power that this demand was met.

13 Angelo and Temptation, I, iii, 52–3

> or that his appetite
> Is more to bread than stone.

Often taken to be a vague allusion to Matthew vii, 9, these lines refer quite clearly to Matthew, iv, 3, where the devil tempts Jesus, saying, 'If thou be the Son of God, command that these stones be made bread.'

The Duke implies that Angelo considers himself, like Christ, to be beyond temptation. Significantly, when Angelo discovers that he is prone to temptation he imagines that Isabella is the devil in disguise (II, ii, 179–81 and II, iv, 16–17).

14 Act II, scene i, lines 39–40

> Some run from brakes of ice, and answer none,
> And some condemned for a fault alone.

Underlying these lines there is a hunting metaphor. Virtue is compared to a stag which makes its way through icy thickets. Some, like Claudio, try to follow its trail, and are punished for a single *fault* (i.e. 'loss of scent', cf. *King Lear*, I, i, 16 where the word 'fault' implies both a physical and a moral deviation from the path of virtue); others, perhaps like Pompey, make no attempt to enter the thickets yet go unpunished. The idea of Virtue passing through a 'brake' occurs both in *Henry VIII*, I, ii, 75–6 'the rough brake/That virtue must go through' and less obviously in *Hamlet*, I, iii, 48 'the steep and thorny way to heaven'.

15 Act III, scene ii, lines 264–85

He who the sword . . . And perform an old contracting. This formal speech (like the song which follows it) helps to separate the harsh realism of the first half of the play from its contrived dénouement. The speech, with its heavily stressed rhythm and end-rhymes and its ritualistic tone, comes appropriately from the Duke, who has performed the role of a chorus throughout the first half of the play and is about to take control of the action. See also *Commentary 16*.

16 Act IV, scene i, lines 60–65

O place and greatness . . . And rack thee in their fancies. These lines would appear to be a part of the Duke's speech at III, ii, 188–95. Here they are neither relevant to their context nor of sufficient length to allow Isabella to inform Mariana of her part in the plot to trap Angelo. It is possible that Shakespeare originally intended the formal speech which now ends Act III to be spoken at this point but that its position was altered to allow for a break in the action. While Mariana and Isabella are conferring it is necessary for the Duke to say something and a make-shift solution would have been to split the earlier speech in two.

17 Act IV, scene iii, lines 1–20

Pompey's list of the prison occupants helps to give the play a flavour of contemporary London. Their names suggest their prevailing vice or folly. *Master Rash* is so called because of his recklessness. *Master Caper* is a gallant who loves dancing. The name 'Dizy' may mean simply 'dizzy' or 'foolish' or it might be a play on the word 'dice'. *Master Deep-vow* may be either a great lover or else a great swearer of oaths. *Master Copper-spur* is probably a social upstart (copper being a base metal). *Starve-lackey* is so called because he does not pay his servant. *Drop-heir* makes a living by exploiting ignorant young heirs. *Forthright* is apparently an aggressive swordsman (*tilter* was a slang term for 'rapier'). *Half-can* seems to have been a dishonest tapster.

SUGGESTIONS FOR FURTHER READING

Articles

R. W. BATTENHOUSE, '*Measure for Measure* and the Christian Doctrine of the Atonment', *PMLA*, lxi (1946), 1029–59.

M. C. BRADBROOK, 'Authority, Truth and Justice in *Measure for Measure*', *Review of English Studies*, xvi (1941), 385–9.

N. COGHILL, 'Comic Form in *Measure for Measure*', *Shakespeare Survey*, viii (1955), 14–27.

Books (most of the following contain only a chapter on *Measure for Measure*)

E. K. CHAMBERS, *Shakespeare: A Survey*. Sidgwick and Jackson (London, 1925); Pelican Books (Harmondsworth, 1964).

R. W. CHAMBERS, *Man's Unconquerable Mind*. Cape (London, 1939).

W. EMPSON, *The Structure of Complex Words*. Chatto and Windus (London, 1951).

G. WILSON KNIGHT, *The Wheel of Fire*. Oxford University Press (London, 1930); Methuen 'University Paperback' (London, 1961).

M. LASCELLES, *Shakespeare's 'Measure for Measure'* (London, 1953).

F. R. LEAVIS, *The Common Pursuit*. Chatto and Windus (London, 1952); Peregrine Books (Harmondsworth, 1962).

A. P. ROSSITER *Angel with Horns*. Longmans (London, 1961).

E. M. W. TILLYARD *Shakespeare's Problem Plays*. Chatto and Windus (London 1950); Peregrine Books (Harmondsworth, 1965).